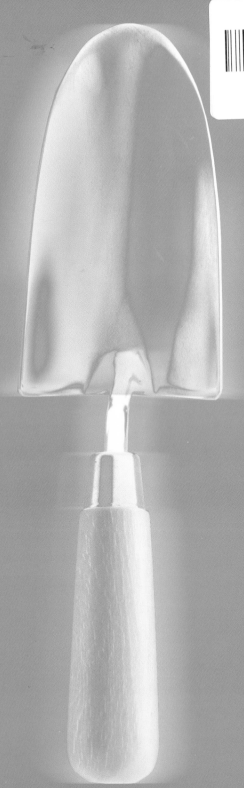

SOMA

how to use this book

The *Gardener's Fact File* is not like other gardening books, and knowing how it works will enable you to get the most of it. This page illustrates some of the kinds of pages that you will come across.

❶ Strategy pages

These guide you through all stages of garden planning, design, planting and maintenance, and point to the right questions to ask yourself to come up with your own solutions.

❷ Directories

These give comprehensive advice on choosing and maintaining materials and features.

❸ Project pages

These use step-by-step photographs to demonstrate essential construction and planting techniques.

❹ Notebook pages

These are interactive, allowing you to fill in and build up your own personal fact file. They provide a place to plan your own garden and space to record inspirations and decisions.

contents

designing
your garden

It's your garden, so you can do what you want – as well as deciding where to grow the Brussels sprouts and put the compost pile, indulge your fantasies and bring your dreams to life. Draftsmanship is useful, but imagination is far more important.

the genius of the place

So you have a garden, and you want to make the most of it. Just where do you begin? You may well come to your new garden full of ideas about what you would like to see, but the reality is that many ideas might be incompatible with the site. The key to successful garden-making is understanding the site – what eighteenth-century landscape architects called "the genius of the place." What does it suggest to you? What are its positive features? What are its drawbacks? Does it have elements that remind you of successful gardens that you have seen and liked?

Often one particular feature dominates a garden, which may seem good or bad at first, but the chances are that you will have to live with it. Let it help you decide how to plan your garden. The garden I have bought recently is on a steep hillside; consequently it has good views, so the design has been determined by the need to develop small, level seating areas, places to appreciate the view, and to create a network

above **Slopes are potentially rewarding places to garden, especially if approached with imagination and a readiness to work harder** than is required on flat land. Here, these old railroad ties have been used to make both terracing and a flight of sturdy steps.

of paths that negotiate the slope to connect the different areas. Planted areas have to look good from above as well as from below. A garden dominated by trees could take "forest" as the theme, perhaps with a log-cabin-type summerhouse, shade-loving plants, and cool leafy planting. A courtyard enclosed by walls, however, may suggest a relatively formal layout, with hints of the Mediterranean or the Middle East.

below **The stark simplicity of arid climates is enhanced by this courtyard planting. It complements the contemporary nature of the architecture, needing little irrigation or upkeep.**

left **A rectangular town garden is echoed in shape by the formality of this design, but any hard edges are softened by luxuriant climbers, especially roses – for which the ample wall space provides a perfect opportunity to clamber.**

first impressions

below **A sunny courtyard evokes the Mediterranean with a selection of perennials, bulbs and patio plants. Steps offer a good opportunity to display containers, although summer watering will be a major task.**

finding potential

What is special about your garden, or potential garden? The first step in design is to analyze the garden's advantages and disadvantages. Remember that it will take a full cycle of seasons before the garden reveals itself completely. Look at your garden carefully and ask yourself some questions.

views

Are there pleasant views? If so, the best place from which to see them could become a good area for relaxing. Is there a distant view, such as distant hills or a townscape? This can be made more of, for example, by framing it in a gap in a hedge or making it visible at the end of a path. Take a photograph of the garden and any view it has, and experiment with covering parts of the view with paper, to help you identify which are worth emphasizing.

climate and aspect

Is your garden predominantly shady or sunny? Talk to previous residents or neighbors to get the full, year-round picture of the sunny and shady areas of your garden. Wherever the sun sets latest in midsummer is an obvious place for a seating or barbecue area. Sunny, open places are important for the more colorful summer plantings and herb gardens and vital for ponds and rock gardens; shadier spots are ideal for spring plantings or cool, secret gardens. Dark, murky corners make useful service areas for compost bins and storage.

gradients

What about the distribution of flat and sloping land? A decent-sized flat area is useful for children's play and large-scale entertaining, but a smaller flat area on a slope has equal potential for smaller gatherings – views up or down add interest.

features

Are there any good aspects to the garden other than plants, such as a fountain, a patio or terrace, an arch or a rock garden? What about practical features, such as a greenhouse or cold frame? Although eventually you may change or move such items, initially you will probably wish to make the most of them.

plants

Are there any good plants, such as established trees, younger trees that might grow to be a major feature, mature shrubs, borders and bulbs? When do existing plants flower or look their best? You may want to add other plants to enhance an already successful planting, or to fill in the gaps, for example, creating an autumn planting around spring-flowering shrubs.

paths

Do the paths direct people around the garden in an interesting way? On a slope, routes are often dictated by the gradient, but on flat land you have more options about where paths should go.

divisions

How is space divided up in the garden? Large gardens may need to be divided to create smaller, more intimate areas. Are you happy with the existing divisions? What is the distinct character of each – open or enclosed, sunny or shaded?

integrated gardens

By now you will be getting a feel for your garden, but before you go any further you need to think about who will be using the space. A garden should serve the needs of all who use it, so the starting point is a list of functions – what and who is the garden for?

▸ Playing. Children need some level areas for games, but love nooks and alcoves and little windy paths. You may want to build a sandbox, treehouse or play structure.

▸ Relaxing. This requires places that invite you to sit and unwind, which could mean enclosed arbors or spots with a lovely view.

▸ Entertaining. A site close to the kitchen can be useful, but you may prefer to put your seating or barbecue where it will catch the evening light in summer.

▸ Viewing wildlife. This entails providing places where wild birds and animals can feel safe to feed and breed, and places from which they can be observed in comfort. A diversity of habitats can be offered by using a wide range of plant shapes and sizes.

▸ Gardening! You will need space for growing the plants you like, whether they are ornamental or edible.

A successful garden is one that integrates as many of the desired functions as possible. Sitting on a patio is all the more enjoyable if the seating area is surrounded by beautiful, fragrant flowers. A pond not only makes an attractive focal point but is also an important wildlife resource.

above **For most people gardens are primarily about relaxation; this sheltered table and chair are a place to escape the sun and seek some serenity among the flowers and foliage.**

✱ **RELATED PAGES**

34 boundaries and divisions

92 entertaining

garden styles

These strong foliage shapes are characteristic of warmer climates and are contrasted with stone. The tank in the center is part of a small water feature.

below **Small spaces are often effectively planted in a formal style – these clipped shrubs and conifers form an evergreen framework, while summer-flowering plants provide bold, if temporary, splashes of color.**

Garden styles are many and varied. They may be partly dictated by the nature of the site – a cold, windswept garden, for example, is likely to feature low-growing heathers and flexible ornamental grasses – or by the forces of history, fashion and taste. Creating a garden in a particular style, or perhaps taking a bit from this and a bit from that, puts an artistic stamp on the plot.

formal gardens

Such gardens put nature at the service of art and are defined by their sense of order and symmetry. They often have clipped hedges in geometric patterns, creating a strong framework. Traditional formal gardens used very few different plants, even filling in the spaces between low hedging with colored gravels. In the twentieth-century English garden style, though, a formal framework is filled in with informal border planting.

informal gardens

These have borders in flowing, curving shapes, and avoid straight lines. Planting can still be planned, with each plant being given its allotted place, and particular species or cultivars grown in clearly delineated blocks. Cottage gardens are an idealized version of country gardens, with an apparently carefree mix of cheerfully flowering plants, giving the impression of spontaneity. Modern European planting design takes this idea further, aiming to capture the feeling of a wildflower meadow in gardenwide swathes of planting.

wild gardens

A further stage in informality encourages wildflower species to flourish, and once they are established maintenance is kept to a minimum, allowing nature to take its course. More minimal still is the marginal garden, where a wild landscape is managed with only occasional mowing and clipping and just a few ornamental species are introduced.

themed gardens

Just as interior designers use paint or wallpaper on the walls, different materials on the floor and furniture, ornaments* and innumerable other things to create a particular atmosphere or ambience in each room, so can the gardener in the garden. And just like indoors, different areas of the garden can be developed following different themes. Particular kinds of plant, surfacing material and container evoke certain feelings, often because of shared cultural associations; bamboo reminds most of us of the Orient, terracotta pots and white walls the Mediterranean, rose arbors romantic English cottage gardens and so on.

Choosing a particular theme is a good way of giving a small garden, patio or courtyard a real stamp of individuality, and little in the way of materials is usually needed. In larger gardens, it is perhaps less easy to keep a theme going. One way in which a theme can be maintained throughout a garden, and throughout the seasons, is by painting wood or metalwork. Using the same color for benches, arches and other structures has a remarkably strong unifying effect on a garden. The use of a particular long-season plant, an evergreen for example, in several different places around the garden also helps to develop a feeling of spatial and temporal continuity.

The easiest way to develop a theme is to feel inspired by what is there already, perhaps turning a "problem" area* into the basis of the theme. For example, plant a hot, dry slope with yuccas and other heat-loving, spiky plants, intersperse these with fragrant lavenders and Mediterranean herbs, add to the seating area some big terracotta containers overflowing with geraniums, and paint a wall white – and you will have given a Spanish or Mexican feel to the garden.

A theme also encourages you to continue developing your garden. You can always be on the lookout for items to add, as well as for suitable plants. A contemporary, yet natural, feel can be evoked by the use of materials such as pebbles or strategically placed pieces of driftwood and railroad ties, combined with lush planting. Every holiday can become a search for things to add to the garden, which will gradually evolve and develop over time.

RELATED PAGES

82 garden ornament

17 problem site analysis

below **A small town garden becomes a dramatic formal space, like a stage set, recalling the influence of theater design on the Italian classical garden tradition.**

developing a style

garden wish list

Most people have a wish list of things they dream about having in a new garden. Thinking about the potential of the site, and getting inspiration from other gardens, will probably mean that this list gets added to: before you know where you are, you have a list of items that a patch of ground four times the size could not accommodate. Now you need to decide what you really want, and when you want it. Start by making lists of everything you (a) have always wanted, (b) did not want initially but think would look good here, and (c) really need.✷ Bearing in mind that there probably will not be room for everything on the list, you need to prioritize.

making a chart

Drawing up a chart (see example below) makes it possible to explore all the different ramifications of your desired garden features. Each feature may perform several different functions, both aesthetic and practical, provide particular opportunities to grow plants and have implications for the overall design of the garden. It should be possible to give everything a priority value. If deciding is difficult, you could give them points out of ten for necessity and for desirability, then add the two figures together. Those with lower figures may have to be scrapped or put off for a future year. Turn to page 26 to fill in the chart for your own garden.

timing of tasks

Once you have decided what there is actually room for in the garden, it is time to decide what needs doing when. Creating a calendar✷ will be helpful. The key points to bear in mind are as follows:

▶ Framework. Structural elements should be established first: paths, axes, trees, main features like ponds, walls and hedges.

▶ Basic essentials. Some tasks, such as creating access paths, must be completed before anything else can be done.

▶ Immediate necessities. Certain things, such as a lawn, may require instant action.

▶ Logical order. Some tasks need to be delayed, as they may get in the way of others; for example, do not begin creating a planted area before you have finished heavy construction.

▶ "Staggering" tasks. Do not attempt to do everything at once, especially if money is tight. Create rough estimates of work at the planning stage.✷

how to decide on features

feature	comments	necessity	desirability	total
Pond	Would provide focal point, and place for children to observe nature	5	8	13
Shed	Essential for storage of tools, outdoor toys, barbecues and chairs	10	8	18
Sandbox	Play space for children and friends' children. Should be located near house	7	9	16

discovering your taste

A good way to discover your own "garden taste" is to visit as many gardens open to the public as possible, and then ask yourself some questions.

▶ List all the gardens that you have visited, or seen photographs of, and liked. What is special about them?

▶ Were they formal or informal? Did they combine elements of both, such as clipped hedging with loose flower borders?

▶ What categories of plant were dominant: trees, shrubs, heathers, perennials, ornamental grasses, summer bedding?

▶ Did nonplant features contribute to the overall feeling – for example, not just the obvious ponds and arches, but the kind of paving used, or the materials used for walls and structures? Were they painted, plain, artificial or natural?

garden moods

Which of the following moods do you like when viewing other gardens?

▶ Intimate/romantic. Spaces enclosed by walls, hedges or large planting; intricate detail that needs time and proximity to appreciate; fragrance.

▶ Grand/expansive. Big views, either to the world outside or within the garden; axes that give views across and through the garden; centerpieces and other features that focus the attention, such as big planters,

symmetrical planting, or formal shapes.

▶ Awe-inspiring. Large, magnificent plants, or plants that look large even if they are not, such as those with big leaves or dramatic, architectural shapes.

▶ Peaceful. Pastel colors; still water; distant views; planting and features that do not try to dominate their surroundings; green foliage.

▶ Dynamic. Lots of large and dramatic foliage shapes, especially spiky ones; a sense of movement.

▶ Mysterious. Odd ornaments; many entrances and exits; nooks and alcoves.

▶ Eccentric. Unusually clipped and trained shrubs; sculptures; bright or startling colors.

▶ Fecund. Lush, luxuriant growth; large plants; masses of flowers; water.

▶ Ascetic. Sparse planting; gravel; the Japanese look; green foliage rather than colorful flowers; minimalism.

▶ Productive. Fruit, vegetables and herbs integrated with flowers.

▶ Wild. Wildflowers; long grass; native plants.

identifying your dislikes

Try to remember all the gardens you heartily disliked, or felt uneasy about, and identify what was wrong with them. Reasons for these feelings about a garden often focus on the following:

▶ Too neat and tidy, or too wild and untidy.

▶ Not enough, or too much messy color.

▶ "Suburban" styles, involving clichéd plants.

▶ "Cluttered," i.e., too much going on.

▶ "Bleakness" i.e., big open spaces.

RELATED PAGES

26 decide what you want

27 your work calendar

30 your garden plan

site conditions

below **Division into four is often the most successful use of a square space. Sun and shade will differ between areas, needing appropriate planting, with shade-tolerant plants for those areas that tend to see less of the sun.**

A garden may have plenty of potential, but it is a rare garden that does not also have some problems, or what may be perceived as problems. A key part of making the most of your garden is to get to know every nook and cranny. Depending on the size of your garden, both soil and microclimate✻ can vary tremendously from one area of your plot to another, with consequences for both human

and plant comfort. It is possible to tell fairly early on where the sunniest and the shadiest places are, but it may take longer to work out where the best shelter is, since wind direction can be unpredictable, or the parts of the garden where the frost lingers longest. Only time will reveal all about your garden, as you find that certain plants thrive in some places and languish in others.

Getting to know the soil will also take time and necessitate some exploratory digging in various places around the garden. The depth of soil often varies, especially where building operations have removed topsoil. The quality can vary greatly too; an area cultivated by previous residents as a vegetable garden may have wonderful, dark, easy-to-dig soil, whereas other areas may be unimproved and heavy. Worst of all, there may be trash and rubble – a common problem in urban gardens.

working with nature

People often think of certain natural conditions as problematic; yet they need not be, if we do not have too inflexible an idea of what we want to grow. It is much easier to work with nature and grow the plants that thrive naturally. There is a wonderful range of beautiful plants that will flourish in many of the conditions sometimes thought of as difficult. Waterlogged areas are marvelous for growing lush bog plants, while thin, dry soils are good for grey-leaved, Mediterranean-type shrubs like lavender; installing drains in the former and importing soil or compost to improve the latter are traditional and expensive options. Only if you want to grow fruit and vegetables do you really need to worry about having top-quality soil. Most ornamentals simply do not need such highly fertile soils to grow reasonably well; indeed, it is often the weeds that benefit most from attempts to improve soil fertility.

As a general rule, plants need light, water and nutrients. A relative lack of one of these is not a disaster; there are specialized plants that will grow in such situations – rhododendrons flourish on poor, acid soils, for example. Such a lack can also be more or less made up for by an abundance of the other two elements; many shrubs that do not normally thrive in shade will do so if the soil is moist and fertile, for example. Where two elements are lacking, however, it will be difficult to persuade anything but the most resilient (and often rather boring) plants to grow; this is why dry shade is one of the most frustrating garden environments.

above **A sunny site and fertile soil are ideal for a vegetable and herb garden. This garden evokes the practical yet carefree atmosphere of the traditional cottage garden.**

✳ **RELATED PAGES**

16 analyzing the site

162 plant selector

analyzing the site

Making a successful garden involves working with what you have as far as possible. It is far less labor-intensive to work with problems on site than to attempt drastic remedies. Choosing plants that will flourish in the prevailing conditions is an important part of this approach. Much can be learned by observing which plants do well locally, in parks and neighbors' gardens. Talking to other gardeners in the area can be a vital source of information. Since different plants have different requirements for light, soil chemistry and climate, knowing the prevailing conditions in your garden will help you make the right choice. It is important to identify your garden's microclimates – individual areas within your garden which vary as to soil and temperature conditions.

sun

If the sun falls onto a wall for most of the day, or onto a bank that slopes towards the sun, it will be hotter there (and the soil drier) than on flat ground – a good site for slightly tender plants or those from Southwestern-type environments.

shade

If there is shade, how deep is it? Does a particular area get sunlight for some of the day, or is the shade dappled, through high tree branches perhaps? If the latter, it may count as "light" or "half" shade, a good place for many herbaceous plants. If soil in shade remains dry for some time after rain has started, or dries out more quickly than soil elsewhere, it is "dry shade," a difficult environment tolerated by relatively few plants.

wind

What happens in the garden during windy weather? Do you have a "prevailing wind," that is one coming mainly from one direction? Go out into the garden during a storm, and note where the wind is strongest and where the sheltered spots are. Sheltered places are best for slightly tender plants and for vegetables. Some maritime areas receive a lot of moist, mild wind, but this is less damaging to plants than a cold wind.

frost

Frost rarely forms in a uniform pattern; often there are areas where it appears more readily than others. Cold air flows like liquid, settling in hollows, and can be dammed by solid objects, resulting in late spring frosts and early autumn ones. Such places need reliably hardy plants and are not suitable for early or tender vegetables, or summer bedding.

soil

▸ How moist is the soil? If water stands around after rain, you have a waterlogging problem; if this occurs frequently or for long periods, only plants from wetland habitats will thrive. If soil dries out quickly after rain, it is probably light and sandy, a soil that usually loses nutrients as quickly as it does water. Most herbaceous plants will grow poorly, but

conditions	nature of problem	drastic remedies	planting solutions
Waterlogging	Many plants drown in wet soil	Drainage (often very labor-intensive and difficult to achieve)	Choose from the wide variety of bog and waterside plants
Heavy clay soil	Soil difficult to work, but usually fertile	Addition of large quantities of compost, gypsum and other soil improvement products (can be labor-intensive and take years to work)	Minimize gardening operations that involve digging – use shrubs and long-lived perennials
Dry or thin soils in hot, dry sites	Many plants suffer from lack of moisture and nutrients	Addition of large quantities of compost to improve soil (quantities may be impractically large); irrigation	Choose from the wide range of drought-tolerant plants; minimize areas of lawn
Thin soils over limestone	Many plants suffer from lack of moisture, and shrubs from nutrient problems	Addition of large quantities of compost to improve soil (quantities may be impractically large)	Choose from the wide variety of smaller perennials, and select appropriate shrubs; minimize areas of lawn
Infertile acid soil	Many plants, especially perennials, suffer from lack of nutrients	Addition of lime and nutrient-rich materials	Choose from the wide variety of acidity-tolerant shrubs
Cold or exposed sites	Frost or wind damage	Use of trees to provide a shelter belt (slow to establish) or fencing	Chose frost- and wind-hardy plants, relying on perennials rather than shrubs

dwarf shrubs and many ornamental grasses will thrive.

▶ Does the soil contain a lot of clay? Clay soils are called "heavy" since they weigh more than other types; they are difficult to work, especially when wet. They are usually fertile, though, and roses and many herbaceous plants will grow particularly well.

▶ Does the soil contain much humus? This is formed from decayed or semidecayed organic matter that holds water and nutrients and plays a major role in plant growth. It gives a characteristic dark color and a friable texture to good-quality topsoil. Lower layers of soil, often left at the surface after building operations have removed the topsoil, are known as "subsoil." This is marked by a reddish, grayish or yellowish color. It lacks humus in any quantity, so you will have to bring in organic material, such as well-rotted manure, in order to improve it.

▶ Is your soil alkaline (limey or calcareous), neutral or acid? Soil-testing kits are readily available. Neutral soils, and those slightly on either side of neutral, are the optimum, allowing you to grow the widest range of plants. Both very alkaline and very acid soils will support attractive ranges of plants, but many garden plants, particularly fruit and vegetables, will not grow well.

The chart above highlights some common garden problems. "Drastic remedies" lists the traditional solutions, which require extensive and often impractical soil alteration. "Planting solutions" focuses on the plants that are naturally adapted to survive in such conditions and which limit extensive, and expensive, work.

surveying your garden

To help you at the planning stage, it is a good idea to make a drawing to scale of your existing garden, so that you know exactly what you are dealing with. Sketch a rough plan while in the garden, then draw it up accurately and neatly later.

below **A rough plan notes all salient facts; anything that affects growing conditions such as shade or waterlogging, as well as the obvious features. Attached notes can be used to record additional information such as the dimension and condition of trees or structures.**

the rough plan

Look at the following aspects of your garden and mark them on your rough plan:

▶ Points of the compass. These will remind you where the sunlight falls, and where prevailing winds come from.

▶ Boundaries and divisions. Note the condition of all boundary or dividing walls, fences and hedges. Are the hedges secure and healthy or are there gaps and occasional dead plants? Will fences and walls need to be repaired or replaced in the near future?

▶ Soil quality. Note any changes around the garden. Very stony, clayey or waterlogged soil should be indicated, or areas full of rocks (often around the house).

▶ Garden structures and buildings. Mark these on the survey with an indication of height. Inspect for signs of weakness, such as decaying lumber or loose stones. Note where the shade falls around a building. Does it get shade all day, or only for a few hours; all year round, or only for a few months? Check for spreading foundations around stone structures. Planting spaces in stone features may be very shallow or may connect with soil underneath; dig or poke around the base to investigate.

▶ Trees. What kind of trees do you have? Are they fully grown? How much bigger are they going to get? Do they look safe and secure? Mark the outline of the canopy of each tree, and the outline of where grass and bare earth meet.

▶ Lawns. Are there patches of poor growth or moss, possibly caused by shade or waterlogging? Old lawns may contain attractive wildflowers – lay off the mowing and see what happens.

▶ Shrubs. Try to identify existing shrubs. How close are they to their mature size?

▶ Flower borders. On site, mark the position of perennials and bulbs with stakes or labels. These plants can often be split and transplanted.

▶ Climbers. Note their position and size. Is there enough space for them when they are mature? If they are growing on supports, are these large or strong enough?

▶ Slopes. Mark the direction and degree of any slopes.

▶ Pools and other water features. Try to establish if they leak. Are they worth keeping? If impossible to remove, how can you make the best of them?

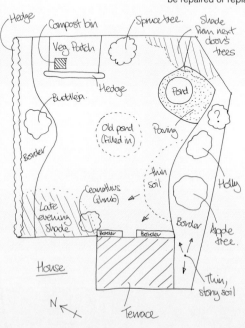

the scale survey

When you have sketched the rough plan, you can then measure up and produce an accurate survey. As equipment you will need (outdoors) two measuring tapes, stakes, clipboard, paper and something with a large right-angled corner to act as a square, and (indoors) graph paper, compasses and ruler.

▶ Attach the rough plan to the clipboard.
▶ Start by measuring the boundaries. Using a stake to hold the end of a measuring tape in place, measure them, and mark the distances on your sketch.
▶ Check that you have drawn in all the features within the garden on the rough sketch and measure the distances between them. Accurately measuring these can be done either (a) by using a base line or (b) by triangulation.
(a) If the garden is roughly rectangular or square in shape, use one of the external boundaries or an obvious axis through the garden as a base line (see diagram above right). First mark the base line using string, chalk or sand. Take a measurement from this line, with your longest measuring tape, out to a feature, creating a side line at a right angle to the base line. Mark where the side line meets the base line and then measure the distance from the beginning of the base line to where the side line meets it. Indicate this on the sketch and repeat the process for each feature.

(b) Triangulation (see diagram below right) is useful for oddly shaped gardens. Choose two base points (A and B) near opposite sides of the garden. Measure the distances between each of the two base points and each feature in the garden, and write these on the sketch as a pair of measurements, always in the same order.
▶ Indoors, transfer your sketch to the graph paper; the markings on the graph paper provide an easy reference for making measurements. Select a simple scale, such as 1in to 1yd, that will allow the scale survey to fit onto the paper with some space around the edges for notes. For (a) above, scale down the measurements from the rough sketch and transfer them to the survey. For (b), first mark down the two base points. Using compasses, for each feature draw an arc at the correct scaled-down distance (use the ruler) from A, and then repeat for B. The point at which the two arcs intersect is the position of the feature.

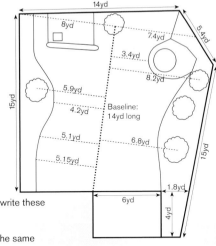

Method (a), using a base line.

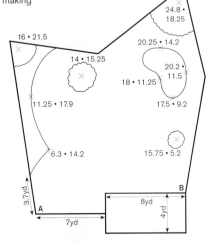

Method (b), triangulation.

planning your garden

The diagrams show two different ways of dividing the space in the same garden. On this page, a new paved area is planned for the sunniest part of the garden. On each side of it there is to be a combination of perennials and ground-cover plants (light shading), those around the oak and pine to include shade-tolerant species, recognizing the fact that the trees are still young. On the other side several shrubs are surrounded by more perennials and ground cover, with a bog garden to one side of the pond (dark shading) and an area of perennial ornamental grass planting around the edge that includes species that look like wetland plants but which are happy on dry land.

Key to shrubs:
1 Ribes sanguineum
2 Deutzia 'Montrose'
3 Exochorda macrantha 'The Bride'
4 Buddleia davidii
5 Salix alba 'Britzensis'
6 Amelanchier lamarckii

It can be difficult to visualize what something will look like from a few lines on paper, but if you have already drawn a survey of your garden, you are well on your way. Then you can start to plan how you want to divide your garden into separate areas, where you want to have planting and where features will be sited.✳ Whether you need to make a plan, and what kind of plan it should be, will depend to a large degree on the extent and complexity of your intended changes to the garden.

willow (cut back)

oak

compost bins

pine

5

pond

1

paved seating area

lawn

3   6
4

cherry

2

terrace

whole-garden plans

A scale drawing of the whole garden will enable you to plan carefully such things as the dimensions of building projects. It is especially useful if you are intending to do much tree planting because you will need to know with a fair degree of accuracy how much the trees are going to impinge on the rest of the garden over the years to come.

area plans

Drawing up plans is also valuable for small areas of planting where it is important to work out which plant will go next to which, and how many are needed. Plans for structural projects such as terraces and ponds are also useful for calculating how much material is needed, how they will fit in with existing elements, and so on.

rough plans

An alternative to an accurately scaled plan is a rough, unscaled plan, which merely represents parts of the garden as a guide, rather than in accurate detail. This can be used to sketch in details of existing features and possible developments, and to make notes on materials needed for a particular project, sources for them, their costs and the timing of work.

visualization techniques

Marking out the garden itself with stakes and strings is a useful adjunct to a plan, and the most graphic way of visualizing ideas for those who do not like pen and paper. It is also a good way to explain ideas to family members. Moving markers around can involve others in

planning. Stakes can be used to mark out the positions of trees and large shrubs, perhaps even color-coded with dabs of paint – blue for conifers, red for flowering shrubs, etc. By using hoses to indicate the outlines of borders, you will be emulating Roberto Burle Marx, one of the twentieth century's greatest garden designers. Other objects, such as slices of logs and flowerpots, may be used to indicate other elements. Whiting (used to mark out recreational courts) can be literally painted onto grass. These graphic markers may be left in place for some time, especially in winter, so that the whole family has plenty of time to consider the proposals.

dividing the space

A crucial part of creating an attractive garden is to divide up the space; there are few gardens duller than those that are visible all at once, that do not invite the adventure of exploration and discovery. There are many ways of dividing up space so that even the very smallest plots can still inspire the sensation of experiencing different atmospheres. The most obvious way of giving each part of the garden a different feel is simply to create "rooms" using walls or hedging; this has been used extensively in many of the classic twentieth-century gardens. Yet it works only in larger gardens; in small ones, the spaces become shaded and oppressive. More subtle and realistic techniques involve partial screens, low hedges, tree or shrub planting, entrances, different surfaces and features that evoke a strong local ambience.

left Gardens that involve geometry need careful planning with pencil and paper and accurate measurements if they are to be successful.

below left In this case the pond has been divided off from the rest of the garden by a low hurdle fence and the area around it developed as a wildlife garden by planting with native shrubs (1) and a wildflower meadow (light shading). Another area nearer the house is sectioned off with low box hedging and used for growing vegetables, herbs, soft fruit and cut flowers. Some vegetables are grown in raised beds. There are access paths made from bark mulch held between planks (dark shading).

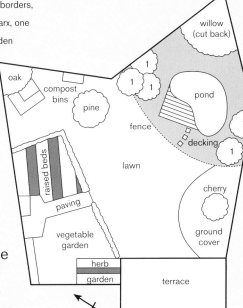

willow
(cut back)
oak
compost bins
pine
1
1
1
pond
fence
decking
1
raised beds
lawn
1
paving
cherry
vegetable garden
ground cover
herb garden
terrace

✳ **RELATED PAGES**

30 your garden plan

organizing the work

when work involves plants; they transplant better at a time when they are more or less dormant and there is little chance of them drying out. It is also easier to visualize structural changes when plants are dormant, without the distraction of foliage and flowers.

timing

Some materials may need to be ordered well in advance of when you intend to start work; this may involve researching sources of supply. Be particularly careful when ordering plants, as they are perishable. Nurseries that offer a mail-order service often only send plants out during the dormant season, and even then sometimes for only a short period, so you may need to order plants months ahead.

professional help

By doing the work yourself in the garden, there is generally less of a chance for things to go drastically wrong than indoors. The exception is electrical work, where a qualified electrician's services are essential. Large projects involving a lot of heavy lifting or specialist machinery are also best tackled by professionals. With any kind of building project, always choose someone who belongs to a recognized trade association.

above **Gardens that involve a lot of hard landscaping materials can be expensive, although recycled materials such as railroad ties can reduce costs, as can doing much of the work yourself.**

Having drawn up a list of projects, prioritized them and planned where they are to go, now consider other factors that might affect when you do them. In cooler climates, although such garden work is usually done in the winter, remember that summer evenings allow you far more time to work outside. Autumn or winter is better for carrying out major work if you live in a hot climate, or

budgeting

Creating a new garden can cost a lot but it can also cost surprisingly little. Shopping around can help a lot. Advertisements in gardening magazines are a useful guide to those companies that offer a mail-order service. Specialized suppliers are often able to offer a more favorable price than nonspecialized local suppliers. Do not forget about nurseries when buying plants, either; they often have a wide range, knowledgeable staff, and reasonable prices. If you need to buy a lot of shrubs for a hedge, for example, try a wholesaler, but you must be sure of what you want. You can even get plants for next to nothing by propagating from your own or friends' existing plants by means of seeds or cuttings. ✳

recycling materials

You can have fun making garden features out of cheap building materials and other people's castoffs. The turf seat on page 56 is an example of the kind of lateral thinking that is the key to recycling.

✳ **RELATED PAGES**

144 Taking cuttings

56 Turf seat

44 Compost bin

left **Investment in attractive and resilient containers is recommended for small urban or roof gardens that need to look near perfect for a long season, and where access might be difficult.**

do it on a budget

project	usual materials	alternatives
Curving metalwork – fences, archways, trellises, etc.	Wrought-iron or other metal. This is expensive to have made to fit and "off-the-shelf" pieces are rarely the right size.	Plastic PVC pipe can be scuffed with sandpaper, painted with weatherproof paint and attached to wooden supports.
Wooden archways, trellises, etc.	Wooden constructions can be bought off the shelf but are often expensive.	Use recycled timber, sanded down and treated with preservative.
Garden benches and seats	Wood or metal furniture is often expensive, and plastic often ugly.	Construct a turf seat. Upright elements in wicker can be added.
Stone troughs (for growing alpines or dwarf plants)	Traditional stone troughs are now very expensive collectors' items.	Cover an ordinary glazed sink with hypertufa (a mixture of cement, soil and sand).
Compost bins, small storage facilities	Usually come ready-made, but rarely the right size for your needs.	Disassembled wooden pallets can be used for many small construction jobs. ✳
Cloches or hot caps (for protecting early or tender plants)	Usually made of glass (which breaks easily) or plastic (which is short-lived).	Use plastic produce baskets such as those used for transporting vegetables, and staple bubble wrap to the frames. Fairly short-lived (two to three years), but very cheap to replace.

planning and cost estimating projects

Whether you go ahead with a garden project or not will depend on both its practicality and affordability. The flow chart below will help you think of all the likely requirements and pitfalls, as well as costs, obvious and hidden. If the cost initially looks too high, consider all the options for each stage before making any final decisions.

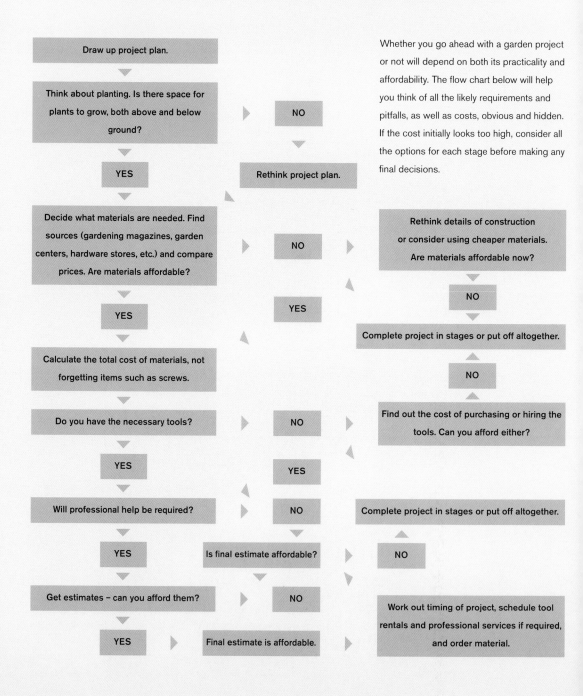

Draw up project plan.

Think about planting. Is there space for plants to grow, both above and below ground?

NO

YES

Rethink project plan.

Decide what materials are needed. Find sources (gardening magazines, garden centers, hardware stores, etc.) and compare prices. Are materials affordable?

NO

YES

Rethink details of construction or consider using cheaper materials. Are materials affordable now?

YES

NO

Calculate the total cost of materials, not forgetting items such as screws.

Complete project in stages or put off altogether.

NO

Do you have the necessary tools?

NO

Find out the cost of purchasing or hiring the tools. Can you afford either?

YES

YES

Will professional help be required?

NO

Complete project in stages or put off altogether.

YES

Is final estimate affordable?

NO

Get estimates – can you afford them?

NO

YES

Final estimate is affordable.

Work out timing of project, schedule tool rentals and professional services if required, and order material.

notebook
designing your garden

This chapter has taken you through the planning process. The following pages provide the space you need to plan the first steps in creating your own garden.

decide what you want

Use this table to compile lists of what you (a) have always wanted, (b) did not want initially but think would look good here, and (c) really need. Some of these features may exist already, but they might be either not to your taste, poorly made or in the wrong place. Note whether you want to keep these features, alter or move them.

feature	comments	necessity	desirability	total

your work calendar

Fill in the details of what you would like, or will have time to do, when. You may find that you have too much work to do in a particular month and you will need to rearrange things. Bear in mind that some tasks are better carried out at specific times of year. See page 22 for advice on timing work.

month	hard landscaping	features	planting
january			
february			
march			
april			
may			
june			
july			
august			
september			
october			
november			
december			

your garden survey

Draw your own garden survey here, following the guidelines set out on pages 18–19.

site survey

site measurements:

aspect:

soil conditions:

weather conditions:

existing features:

existing planting:

address book:

your garden plan

Draw your own garden plan here, following the guidelines set out on pages 20–21. For space to plan individual elements of your garden in more detail, use the notebook in the next chapter, "Developing a Framework."

garden plan

landscaping materials:

structures and features:

planting:

address book:

developing
a framework

A garden can stand or fall by its structural elements. They make a statement all through the year, even in winter when there's not much else happening in the garden. Time and effort spent getting the garden framework right will be amply rewarded.

boundaries and divisions

as the need to create a screen against noise, the wind, or an ugly view. The decision about how to mark a boundary can arouse strong feelings because it affects more than one household: a hedge of young trees may grow to be a monster that denies your next-door neighbor any view of the sun. Fences and walls at least do not grow, but your neighbors are surely entitled to some say in the matter.

internal divisions

Internal divisions, used to separate one part of the garden from another, are created with a different purpose in mind. Where an external boundary may be erected to provide security and privacy, internal divisions often fulfill the purpose of enticing the visitor to venture further into the garden.

simple screens and barriers

One part of the garden may be screened off simply by planting a shrub – indeed, breaking up space is one of the essential attributes of shrubs in the garden. By hiding whatever is behind it, the question of what is there is immediately raised in the mind of the onlooker. A trellis is also an effective screen, taking up minimal horizontal space and allowing limited and enticing views through it. Climbers will enhance its decorative value and add to its screening properties.✻

Low hedges may not offer a physical barrier to views across the garden, but they do create an equally important psychological

above Walls make for a very definite and solid boundary, but one that can be softened with a trellis and climbers. Walls are particularly useful for reflecting the heat of the sun, which many plants will appreciate.

external boundaries

Because they delineate and divide territory, boundaries tend to excite strong feelings. There are, for example, sharply opposing views about whether they should be emphasized or played down. Some feel that "Good fences make good neighbors" and others that "It is unfriendly to create barriers." More practical issues may be apparent, such one, because they force the viewer to proceed in a particular direction. Dwarf box (*Buxus sempervirens* 'Suffruticosa') and lavender (*Lavandula*) are two of the most effective and popular plants used for this purpose. Traditional uses for these plants include the division of vegetable beds and herb gardens.

subtle divisions

Even without any sort of barrier, it is possible to differentiate one part of a garden from another by creating some sort of obvious entrance. Archways, usually draped with climbers, are very popular for this purpose, their role in the garden being very much like that of a doorway into a room. Simpler still is an entryway formed by a pair of identical compact shrubs, perhaps clipped into standards, with an obvious path between them. Different ground coverings are another way of subtly separating one part of the garden from another; the transition of stepping from grass onto paving, for example, instantly creates the sensation of entering another space. When allied with a low hedge or wall or some other marker, this effect becomes even stronger.

left **A low hedge forms a psychological boundary, separating one part of the garden from another without creating a physical barrier. Lavender is ideal for this purpose but needs clipping every year after flowering in order to stay tidy.**

 RELATED PAGES

78 the vertical dimension

directory: walls and fences

natural stone wall

walls

Wall design demands some thought with regard to the grand plan of the garden. Walls are the most costly method of enclosing and defining spaces and provide security, privacy and shelter. Professional advice should be sought on retaining walls and on freestanding walls over 3ft. Building materials include bricks, concrete blocks, and natural or reconstituted stone, and should reflect those already used in the locality.

Constructing walls is a skilled job that necessitates the use of a level and line to ensure that each course is completely level. A mortar mix of 1:6

(soft sand to cement) is standard, although a coarse sand and a firmer mix is often used with natural stone. The wall is pointed as the mortar dries; different styles of pointing can contribute character to the finished wall.

Foundation width is generally twice that of the wall. A minimum depth of 6in of concrete supports a wall up to 3ft high.

Copings protect the top of a wall from penetration by water and an overhang helps shed water from the wall face. Bricks can be used to make a coping course, but flat slabs or coping stones are the easiest and cheapest to lay.

Maintenance of well-constructed walls is unnecessary unless painted, when a fresh coat every two to four years suffices. Old walls may need repointing after first raking out all the joints deeply.

brick walls The beautiful patterned texture of brick walls is enhanced by the bond (the pattern in which the bricks are laid) and color variation between bricks. Wire-cut clay bricks have a more modern appearance than

many molded ones, but both will mellow with weathering. Concrete bricks are less likely to age well. For retaining walls it is essential to use frost-resistant bricks.

block walls Larger concrete blocks are cheap and quick to lay, and their appearance can be improved by rendering and painting the finished wall. Reconstituted stone block is available in various sizes and finishes at relatively low cost.

rendered wall with coping

brick wall

natural stone walls Walls built of rubble stone are labor-intensive. Ashlar stone is shaped or "dressed" and, although more expensive to buy than rubble, is quicker and easier to build with. If only one wall face is visible, cut costs by using stone as a veneer to concrete block.

ornamental panel fencing

fences

Fences are cheaper than walls but less durable. If made so that they filter the wind, they reduce the problems of turbulence sometimes encountered behind solid walls. Most fences are vulnerable to wind, so an investment in good construction is worthwhile if the site is at all exposed.

The basics of construction are similar for most types of fence. For post-and-rail fences the posts may be driven directly into the ground, and the rails nailed to the posts. For other types of fence the posts are set in concrete and braced upright until the concrete is set. Pressure-treated posts have a life of 15–20 years. Metal post socks are an alternative to concrete but are difficult to drive into stony ground and seldom secure unless concreted too. Concrete posts last but are unattractive. Bundles of wood can be gathered together and attached so that the posts are invisible on one side.

The weakest point of any fence is the part below ground, so repeated applications above ground of preservative, stains or paints are essentially cosmetic only.

post-and-rail fences These are the quickest and cheapest type of fence to erect, but they provide no privacy.

panel fences Panels are usually supplied in 6ft widths and various heights, and the range available includes basketweave, interwoven, lattice, louver and picket.

close-board fences These are strong and solid, made from overlapping vertical boards fixed to a post-and-rail structure.

mesh fences These offer security, but no privacy. Climbers grown up a mesh fence can turn it into a fedge – a cross between a fence and a hedge.

hurdles

hedges

hedges

Unlike walls and fences, hedges have the advantage of being self-repairing. They can also provide better wind protection: by filtering the wind rather than acting as a solid barrier, turbulence on the leeward side is reduced.

H = Height after five years

P = Planting distance of young plants

formal hedges are clipped into geometric shapes, like green walls. Only trees with dense growth and small leaves are suitable, the most popular being as follows:

Boxwood *(Buxus sempervirens)* is an evergreen, bushy shrub with elegant, narrow foliage. A slow grower, it is most effective when used for low hedges or creative topiary effects. *Cultivation*: Sun or semishade, and any soil except waterlogged ones. Prune in late spring. H: 3ft P: 1ft

Hornbeam *(Carpinus betulus)* makes an effective windbreak and is a good choice for autumn color, with elegant dark green leaves which turn yellow and orange. *Cultivation*: Sun or semishade on well-drained soil. Tolerates clay soil and windy sites. H: 6½ft P: 1ft

laurel hedge

European beech *(Fagus sylvatica)* is a slender tree whose oval leaves turn yellow and orange-brown in autumn. It makes a good windbreak, although it can be slow and difficult to establish. *Cultivation*: Full sun and well-drained soil. H: 5ft P: 1ft

Privet *(Ligustrum ovalifolium)* has a neat habit and withstands clipping well. *Cultivation*: Sun or semishade and any well-drained soil. Prune in midspring. H: 10ft P: 1ft

Honeysuckle *(Lonicera nitida)* is a vigorous, evergreen shrub with a neat habit that can be used as a faster-growing alternative to box. *Cultivation*: Fertile, well-drained soil in sun or semishade. H: 5ft P: 20in

yew hedge

English yew *(Taxus baccata)* is a relatively fast-growing, upright conifer, making an elegant, traditional hedge that is a good background for colorful planting effects. It is also suitable for creative topiary effects. *Cultivation*: Sun or semishade, on any well-drained soil, including chalk. H: 5ft P: 20in

informal hedges are those where plants are allowed to develop a more natural form and pruned only when they become too large or ragged. A variety of shrubs can be used: spiny varieties are useful for security purposes, and flowering ones for ornamental value.

Barberry *(Berberis thunbergii)* has sharp spines, attractive foliage and, in winter, scarlet berries. *Cultivation*: Sun or semishade in any well-drained soil. H: 5ft P: 16in

Single seed hawthorn *(Crataegus monogyna)* is the mainstay of country hedges. It is fast growing, with flowers, berries and spines. *Cultivation*: Prefers full sun but tolerates almost any conditions except very wet soil. H: 5ft P: 1ft

Escallonia species are good for coastal areas. *Cultivation*: Full sun; fertile, well-drained soil. Prune after flowering. H: 6½ft P: 20in

Fuchsia is good in mild regions. *F. magellanica* or *F.* 'Riccartonii' are both

Berberis thunbergii **hedge**

suitable. *Cultivation*: Sun; well-drained soil. H: 8ft P: 20in

Rosa rugosa makes a dense hedge, with attractive flowers followed by red hips. *Cultivation*: Prefers sun, and moist but well-drained soil. Prune in early winter. H: 5ft P: 20in

Tamarix gallica, with its feathery foliage and pink flowers, makes a good hedge in coastal areas. *Cultivation*: Sun; fertile, well-drained soil. H: 5ft P: 1ft

fuschia hedge

what goes where

Think of the garden as comprising three zones – inner, middle and outer – radiating out from the house. Each zone has its own character and function, which should be considered when you are deciding where to situate each feature in your garden. The further out the zone is, the less it is likely to be used. Very small gardens may have only the inner zone, whereas only larger ones have an obvious outer zone.

inner zone

Literally a few steps from the house, this is the area of domesticity and high visibility, so treat the following as priorities.

▸ Enjoying plants. Decorative planting needs to look good for as long as possible.

▸ Entertaining. This is the obvious place for entertaining, close to the house and the kitchen. However, it may make more sense to locate the terrace further from the house if you want to enjoy the view of a feature such as a pond elsewhere in the garden.

▸ Play. A sandbox or other area designed for smaller children needs to be near the house where they can be watched with ease.

▸ Kitchen garden. Fresh herbs and salad vegetables should ideally be grown close to the kitchen door, but since most of them need full sun, this may not always be possible. ❋

middle zone

This zone is characterized by ornament and space. Think about how you wish to use it.

▸ Borders and other plantings. A long season of interest may be desirable, but it is perhaps less important in the middle zone than right next to the house.

▸ Grassed areas. Lawn or some area of grass is essential for children's games, sunbathing, or partying. If these are not important to you, consider whether you actually want an area of grass here. You might prefer growing plants, being a gardener rather than a groundsman. If your middle zone is mainly in the shade, remember that grass needs sun and rapidly dries out in shade. Such areas should either be planted with shade-loving plants, or screened off and treated as part of the outer zone.

▸ Decorative features. Ponds, archways, arbors, rock gardens and all the other features that add interest to a garden are ideally situated in the middle zone. You may want to link them or have them close to a terrace in the inner zone. Think about how structures such as archways and trellises supporting climbers can be used as a transition between the inner and middle zones. Remember, however, that nearly all these features need sun for most of the day to be a success.

below **In warm climates, seating areas are best located in a cool and shady area of the garden, which is often a good place for some of the best foliage plants.**

upright cupboards, made of glass or clear plastic, they are designed to be attached to a fairly sunny wall.

▸ Garden waste. The outer zone is a good place for a compost bin, if you decide you need one. Really good compost is produced when bacteria cause a pile to heat up, killing fungal diseases and weed roots and seeds. You need at least 3cu. ft of compostable material to get this reaction going, so this is only really practicable for larger gardens.

▸ Fruit and vegetables. Vegetables often undergo an unsightly phase that you may want to hide. A small orchard is a good way of using more distant space.

▸ Wildlife. The quiet further reaches of the garden can be a terrific benefit for wildlife, especially if the zone links with similar areas in neighboring gardens.✳ Maintenance needs will be minimal for native shrubs and rough grass.

RELATED PAGES

150 gardening to eat

96 features for wildlife

left **A paved area provides a transition between the house and a lawned area beyond.**

below **Attractive compost bins like this do not have to be hidden from view, but should not be placed too close to the house.**

outer zone

Areas that are a long way from the house, screened off from the rest of the garden, or not easily accessible, can be used for practical functions or as a wilderness area.

▸ Storage. A spacious, waterproof shed is useful to store tools, seeds and equipment. If space is limited, it makes more sense to buy a secure cabinet that can be attached to a wall or hidden away in a corner.

▸ Greenhouses and cold frames. You may want to raise your own bedding plants from seed, or grow tender fruits and vegetables like tomatoes and cucumbers. Cold frames and greenhouses should be sited in a sunny, sheltered part of the garden. Mini-greenhouses are also available. Resembling

project: sandbox

Sandboxes are most fun if they are large enough for children to climb into with their friends. This sandbox is made from two wooden frames, one on top of the other. Make the bottom frame deeper, if you want a greater depth of sand.

tools • spade • hammer

materials • crushed stone (¾in) • water-permeable membrane • pressure-treated timber: 4 pegs, 2 x 2 x 7in; 4 pegs, 2 x 2 x 5in; 8 planks of 6 x 1½ x 60in • nails • hooks • sand

1 Dig a ditch slightly larger than you want your finished sandbox to be and 10in deep, if you want a semisunken sandbox. Fill the bottom with a level 3in layer of crushed stone to provide drainage for the pit.

2 Using four of the pressure-treated planks, and with a long peg at each corner, make a square base frame to contain the sand. Nail a water-permeable liner to the bottom of the frame to make a floor, ensuring that no dangerous nail heads stick out.

4

Keeping the sand in a sandbox clean is as important as keeping the area around the sandpit neat. Keeping the sandbox covered is the only way to ensure that the sand stays clean for your children. Hard covers for large sandboxes are not only difficult to make and fit but are awkward to move and store. Trailer suppliers will make covers to order in canvas or PVC, fitted with eyelets and elastic rope which will drop over the hooks on the frame for a snug fit.

Then, if you pave around a fixed sandbox and you use our model, you can easily remove the top frame from time to time to allow you to sweep any clean sand spills directly back into the box.

It is easy to remove both sand and wooden frames when your children outgrow the sandbox, and to install another feature: you already have a hole, so turning it into a small pond would be easy.

3 Position this first frame in the crushed stone so that its top sits fractionally below the surrounding border. If you want a removable top tier like ours, make another, identically sized frame with the remaining four planks and the short corner pegs; fit this over the outstanding pegs of the first frame for a solid fit. Then add timber braces at each corner – to help keep the structure stable, and to provide seating. Lastly, attach hooks to the outside of the upper tier; a canvas cover can then be attached to these.

4 When you fill the sandbox, use silver sand or other coarse sand – not pit sand or builder's sand, which is very fine and can stain clothing. Fill the box to a depth of only 6in and, using the top frame as a rim, you will minimize the amount of sand spilled unnecessarily. Finally, to add extra solidity to the structure, fill any crevices outside the frame with gravel.

project: compost bin

You can make a compost bin for next to nothing – using old wooden pallets. Your bin must have a capacity of at least 35cu. ft in order to stimulate the high-temperature decaying process needed for efficient compost production.

3

1

2

tools • saw • hammer • 3in paintbrush

materials • 2 wooden pallets • 4 wooden posts, 2 x 2 x 36in • 4 wooden battens, ½ x ½in x 3ft • clear wood preservative • galvanized nails

1 Dismantle the pallets and then saw the planks into lengths. Our compost bin requires 30 lengths of 3ft, 10 each for the sides and back, and 10 slightly shorter lengths, which will slot in to form the front. Lay all the planks, together with the four corner posts and the battens, on the ground; brush each piece with preservative and leave to dry.

Build one of the side panels: lay two uprights on the ground and nail 10 planks to them, flush with the outside edge of the upright and to each other. Make the second side in the same way.

4

compost material

Efficient high-temperature composting depends on a good mixture of fresh, soft material, such as grass clippings, and harder remains – from perennials and vegetables. You can compost any nonwoody organic material, but avoid meat or fish waste, and large quantities of starchy root vegetable waste, because these will attract rats before they start to decay. When the bin is full, take everything out, mix it up and then put it back. This will aerate it, initiating a highly active decay process, and producing enough heat to kill weed seeds and pests. When the pile begins to cool down again, repeat this turning process to restimulate the composting process.

2 Turn over the two side panels and make the channels for the removable slats. On the upward-facing side of the post that will be at the front of the compost bin, nail into place two wooden battens, sawn to length and far enough apart to accommodate the front slats. Then add a third short piece between these two at ground level, to form an end stop.

3 Stand the two side panels up to build the back panel. Nail one of the remaining 10 planks across from one side panel to the other at the top to hold them together. Next nail the bottom plank in position, and then fill in the middle; in this way, the bin stays square.

4 Turn the bin the right side up and place it in position. (To be sensible, this should be somewhere easily accessible, so that throwing waste into the bin does not become a chore.) Slot the front slats into the channels on the uprights and slide them down into place. Finally, nail one longer plank across the top between the two uprights; this will square up the whole structure and help to keep it stable.

hard surfaces

A hard surface, such as concrete, has many advantages in a garden, as it does not get muddy and is easily swept clean. It does not need mowing like a lawn, dramatically reducing maintenance. Most gardens have a patio or terrace – a place to put a table and chairs and not worry about them sinking into the lawn. In many gardens this will be the focus of the whole project, the spot from which the garden will be seen and admired the most.❋ In very small gardens it may occupy a considerable proportion of the garden, perhaps even taking the place of the traditional lawn, with borders of plants coming right up to the edge.

Hard-surfaced paths are often a great advantage because they can be used as much as necessary in wet weather without damaging the surface. On heavy soils, where muddy soil clings to boots and wheelbarrow wheels and clogs gravel or other loose materials, they are an absolute must. They are also useful on slopes where sliding is a possibility in the wet.

choosing materials

The material from which a hard surface is made is of crucial importance. These surfaces are not just for convenience, but play a key role in the overall appearance of the garden because they act as a contrast to lawn or borders and are strikingly obvious all year long. Compromising on your choice of materials may be a mistake you will have to live with for a long time, especially since

left **Old railroad ties are some of the most attractive and useful of recycled materials. The bricks here are reused paving – the lines on them reduce the dangers of slipping.**

many hard surfaces can involve considerable investment. This is even more so in small gardens where the proportion of hard to other surfaces is high.

When selecting materials for a hard surface, the first factor is simply whether you like them or not; consider them first in isolation, and then in context with your house and other hard surfaces in the garden, such as walls. You may find yourself seeing the material in two very different lights. Compared with almost anything else you do in your garden, a mismatch between the material of your house, and most likely the rest of the neighborhood, and a hard surface in the garden is going to stand out.

Paving slabs are the obvious hard surface to many; cheap ones, however, usually look cheap, and good ones can cost a lot. Bricks are a popular alternative – old ones can be cheaper and carry a patina of age. Brick ends and pavers are thinner than bricks, being made specifically for paving. These smaller-sized materials are easier to manage than slabs and can be arranged into interesting patterns.

Decking is a wooden alternative to paving, with a softer, more natural look, which suits some gardens better than stone or brick surfaces.✳ It also has the immense advantage that, when properly supported, it can be used to build out over slopes or water.

far left **This is a most unusual surface, combining the appearance and qualities of lawn and paving. Small, creeping flowering plants could also be used here instead of grass. All power to the imagination!**

  RELATED PAGES

50 decking

directory: hard surfaces

gravel and decking

construction

Washed and graded gravel, ½–¾in in size, is ideal and should be laid in a ¾in-thick layer over a compacted subbase of scalpings, or binding ballast. The base should be 3in deep for paths or 6in deep for driveways. An edging restraint of either pressure-treated lumber or mortared brick is advisable.

gravel

Gravel is one of the cheapest and easiest choices for hard surfaces in the garden. The noise it makes when walked on means that it is a good option for the security conscious. It should not be laid in too deep a layer because it will hamper walking or get scattered by vehicles. An enormous range of colors is available, but a local quarry will be the cheapest source and may even be able to match the local colors too. River or pit gravels are rounded and often more attractive than gravels crushed from quarried rock.

paving slabs, bricks

These may be natural materials, for example stone or clay, or less expensive alternatives such as reconstituted stone or precast concrete. Natural stone paving may be irregular both in outline and in depth and consequently more time-consuming to lay. Concrete slabs may have a very plain finish (pressed, polished or aggregate-exposed), but more expensive ranges include molded finishes with subtle color variations which can resemble real stone. An uneven edge and variety of sizes, giving a random pattern when laid, can result in an interesting and natural look.

construction For hard-wearing paving, slabs should be laid on a bed of 1:6 mortar mix over a compacted 3in deep base of crushed stone. If the slabs are butted close together, pointing is unnecessary.

flexible paving

Flexible paving – an interlocking pattern of units laid within rigid edging restraints – is a durable and easily maintained surface, and is ideal for steep inclines which would shed gravel. Bricks and setts are available in a great range of colors and finishes including rumbled units, which provide an instant, distressed surface.

construction Edging restraints, flush or raised, must be rigid on a concrete footing; curb units are

bricks

appropriate for driveway edges. Interlocking clay or concrete bricks or setts are laid dry onto a bed of sand 20in deep over 4in depth of compacted subbase. Set the brick into place with a rubber mallet and brush dry sand into the joints.

is red cedar, which is naturally very durable. Most softwoods must be pressure-treated for longer life.

construction Wooden slats, usually 3 x 1in, are fixed using galvanized nails onto a supporting framework of posts, beams and joists.

maintenance of surfaces

Slabs and bricks that become green and slippery can be washed down annually using a high-pressure jet or stiff brush and algicide or cleaner, taking care with neighboring plants.

Mortar coming loose from joints should be raked out and renewed. Gravel paths, flexible paving and unpointed paving all suffer from weed growth, which can be controlled by an annual application of a herbicide in spring. Gravel traps dirt gradually and renewal of the top layer every few years will keep it looking fresh.

Painted or stained lumber may require a fresh coat every two to four years. Whether stained or not, decking benefits from an annual rinse with a high-pressure jet. Pressure-treated lumber and red cedar require no repeat treatment with a preservative.

decking

decking

Decking is warm underfoot and ideal for dry climates and sunny situations where timber does not attract algal growth and become slippery. It is the ideal solution for a level seating area on sloping ground, since expensive foundations and retaining walls are unnecessary. The most expensive timber for decking

gravel

project: decking

3

Lumber decking is an increasingly popular alternative for paving on a terrace or patio. If you use a hardwood, you should ensure that it comes from a renewable source; if you use a less expensive softwood, it should be pressure-treated.

1

2

tools • saw • level • screwdriver • nail gun/hammer

materials • right-angled brackets • 2 x 2in pressure-treated lumber for supporting joists • 4 x ½ x 60in decking planks

1 Calculate how much lumber you will need as accurately as possible before you start; it is perhaps easiest to draw a plan to scale and hand it to your lumber salesperson. Then lay a crisscross framework of joists over the area to be decked, close enough together not to test the strength of the decking planks. Use a level to check whether the frame is level and position bricks or blocks of wood under the joists that are too short, to lift them to the appropriate height. Secure with right-angled brackets. If you are not covering a raised patio as we did, a level layer of compacted crushed stone laid on firm

why wood?

Softer in appearance than paving stones or brick, decking provides a sympathetic transition between house and garden, its straightedged linearity echoing the architecture's strong lines, while its natural texture blends comfortably with the softer lines of plants in the garden beyond. Wood has a naturally warm character which is more welcoming than stone in anything cooler than midsummer. It also weathers very attractively, as the harder grain in the wood becomes more exposed. Wood is also a very flexible medium: it is easy to cut, which makes decking the ideal choice for an awkwardly shaped site, and you can paint it for a bolder statement.

subsoil will provide a suitable foundation, few patios being required to support heavy loads.

2 Position your planks from the house outwards. Position the first plank flush with the doorway; it is easier to trim the outside edge of your outermost plank than to accurately saw the final plank to fill a gap between the rest of the deck and the house. Leave a $^3/_8$in gap between each plank to allow for a little movement in the timber – and for drainage.

3 Saw your planks into lengths that correspond to the positioning of your joists, so that all the joints lie directly over a supporting joist. Make sure that the joints are staggered from row to row, herringbone fashion.

4 For speed, use a nail gun to secure your planks to the joists. Use galvanized nails; alternatively, decking screws would fix the planks even more firmly, and an electric drill fitted with a screwdriver head makes the job relatively painless.

soft surfaces

Mown grass forms the central part of many gardens, especially larger ones.* It has many advantages for family gardens: it is a soft surface to lie or fall onto, and it makes a splendid foreground to surrounding planting. Its disadvantages are the amount of maintenance it needs, even if all you ever do is mow it, and the fact that in dry summers it turns brown. In areas where water conservation is a high priority, this can become a major problem. Remember, also, that grass does not grow in any but the very lightest shade. Lower-maintenance options for soft surfaces include the use of other ground cover plants, and areas of gravel or bark chips used as a mulch and interspersed with herbs and flowers, which can make a pleasant change from grass.

below **Long grass is one of the most romantic and gentle of all surfaces in the garden. Interesting design effects can be achieved by surrounding or intersecting an area of long grass with paths of more regularly mown grass.**

grass lawns

Grass is sold as either seed or turf. Seed comes in two basic types: one with rye grass and one without. The former, once grown, is coarse in appearance but wear-resistant, which is essential in places that are going to receive regular use, such as play areas. The latter is composed of fine-leaved, slower-growing species that create a much better looking, but less resilient, surface. Turf is instant in effect, but works out to be considerably more expensive. Turf is usually of the rye grass kind; fine-leaved turf generally has to be specially ordered and costs more.

long grass

A recent revival of interest in wildflowers and the encouragement of wildlife in the garden has focused interest on the possibilities of unmown or only occasionally mown grass, particularly in the further reaches of the garden, if it is a large one. Long grass, with or without wildflowers, can be very attractive, giving a soft and varied texture quite distinct from that of mown grass. Mown paths through the long grass make it look intended, rather than unkempt, and add to its romantic appeal. Mowing need only be done a few times each year.

ground cover plants

Some ornamental ground cover plants offer an attractive alternative to grass, usually because they are more drought resistant or

left Periwinkle *(Vinca major)* is used here as ground cover on a slope – the ideal solution to an area that would otherwise be difficult to plant.

grow better in shade. Different species or cultivars can also be combined to form patterns. None need the amount of maintenance that grass does – just occasional weeding rather than regular mowing – and many of them flower or have attractive foliage, both good reasons for their increasing popularity. With the exception of the traditional chamomile lawn, hardly any of these ground cover plants can be walked on regularly, which limits their value as a direct replacement for lawn grass. Many lawns receive little regular foot traffic, however – perhaps only when they are being mown! Ground cover plants are particularly useful on slopes and banks. One option is to use grass for heavily used footpaths and ground covers for other rarely used areas.

gravelled areas

Gravel is an alternative to grass, and when combined with plants growing up through it from the soil beneath makes a fashionable soft surface. An impermeable layer of plastic is often placed between the gravel and the soil to limit weed invasion, with holes cut in them for the plants to grow through. The results are low maintenance and often highly successful, with the gravel providing a good foil to flower and foliage color.

 RELATED PAGES

10 garden styles

58 gravel garden

directory: soft surfaces

bark chips

The choice of soft surface will depend on whether you are planting for effect or for ease of maintenance. Some soft surfaces, such as bark chips, also act as a mulch, while others, such as some ground cover plants, will act as weed suppressors.

ground cover materials

Bark or wood chips make an attractive and natural-looking soft surface, but can be expensive if a bulk source is not located. Beware of very fresh coniferous material as this may damage perennials. Chips should be laid in a layer 2in thick.

Shredded garden waste from twigs and woody materials makes a cheap, natural-looking surface, although because it is short-lived, it needs to be replaced fairly often. Lay in a 2in-thick layer.

Coconut shells, laid in a 3in-thick layer, look very neat. Unfortunately, they are expensive and ecologically dubious; they are also something of an acquired smell.

Gravel used as a mulch makes an attractive soft surface that keeps the roots of plants cool. Lay in a 2in-thick layer. It makes a poor weed suppressor unless used in conjunction with another less permeable soft surface, such as black plastic.

ground cover planting

The cost of using ground cover as an alternative to grass is perhaps one of the main reasons why it is not more popular with amateur gardeners. Even if the plants are bought wholesale, the cost soon mounts. Many ground covers are easily propagated, however, and it may be worth spending several years propagating plants in order to be able to achieve a successful result. Ground covers should leave no gaps when complete, so choose plants that will thrive in the given conditions.

H = Height

S = Spread after three years

chamomile lawn

Lamium maculatum

shade, and all soils including dry ones. Propagate by division. H: 2ft S: 20in

Chamaemelum nobile (chamomile) has aromatic, feathery foliage and bears small white flowers in summer. It is tolerant of foot traffic. *Cultivation*: Full sun, including dry areas. Propagate by seed or division. H: 8in S: 16in

Hedera helix (ivy) has dark green, glossy, evergreen leaves and insignificant flowers; other varieties of ivy are equally suitable. All tolerate a limited amount of foot traffic. *Cultivation*: Shade, including deep and dry shade. Propagate by division, if necessary; it self-roots easily. H: 4in S: 2ft

Hypericum calycinum has leathery, semievergreen leaves and large yellow flowers in summer. It does not tolerate foot traffic. *Cultivation*: Sun or light shade, and all soils including acid ones. Propagate by division. H: 1ft S: 2ft

Lamium galeobdolen has semi-evergreen, silver-splashed foliage and yellow flowers in spring. It does not tolerate foot traffic. *Cultivation*: Shade. It can be propagated by division, but self-roots easily and can even be invasive. H: 8in S: 3ft

Achillea millefolium (yarrow) has dark, feathery, semievergreen foliage and white flowers in summer. It has limited tolerance of foot traffic and acts as a weed suppressant. *Cultivation*: Sun or light shade. Propagate by division. H: 16in S: 16in

Alchemilla mollis has elegant, light-green foliage with sprays of lime-green flowers in early summer. It does not tolerate foot traffic, but does act as a weed suppressant. *Cultivation*: Sun or light shade. Propagate by division. H: 1ft S: 20in

Carex pendula has dark green, straplike, evergreen leaves and bears pendent catkins in summer. Does not tolerate foot traffic. *Cultivation*: Sun or

Hedera helix

project: turf seat

Particularly suitable for gardens that lie on a slope, a turf seat is an attractive and inexpensive alternative to conventional garden furniture – or to the more fragrant chamomile seat. It creates a romantic feature, particularly when surrounded by wildflowers in a secluded corner.

tools • spade • sharp knife • pruners

materials • bamboo poles • turf

1 Excavate the bank to the depth you wish the seat to be and wide enough to accommodate two people comfortably. Do not hurry this stage, because if you dig out too much soil, it will be very difficult, if not impossible, to replace it securely. Be careful to remove any sharp or large stones at this point as well, since they will make the seat uncomfortable, which defeats the object of the exercise.

2 Choose a seed-grown turf which will be a suitable environment for wildflowers too, ideal if you are looking for an attractive and low-maintenance framework for your feature. Roll out the turf on your seat, pushing it hard into the

sides to make good contact with the soil underneath, thereby encouraging good rooting. Then, to hold it in place, hammer bamboo poles through it into the earth at the sides.

3 Once the sides are secure, cut off any of the bamboo poles which have hit against rocks or roots, and are therefore sticking out, with pruners as close to the surface of the soil as possible, making sure that they are not going to stick into the backs of future visitors.

4 Your rolls of turf will most likely not fit the dimensions of your seat exactly, but you can easily cut the turf to size using a sharp knife. Use small strips to fill in any awkward gaps. Water the seat regularly during the first few weeks, especially if the weather is dry, in order to help the root system get established. To make the feature look established as quickly as possible, you should plant the surrounding area at the same time. Wildflowers and aromatic plants such as primulas, campanulas and thyme will make for attractive surroundings.

placement

When you are planning where to put your turf seat, you will probably be constrained by the physical contours of your garden, but if you have a number of choices, you should consider whether it is possible to position it to catch the morning or evening sun, for instance, depending on when you are most likely to use the seat. Decide whether to site it under a tree that will provide partial shade, or in full sun if you are a sun lover. Consider whether you would like the seat to become a focal point, or whether it can be tucked out of sight as a retreat from the main avenues of the garden, somewhere to sit quietly and read, perhaps.

project: gravel garden

Gravel is not only useful for paths: when used as a mulch it keeps the soil cool and moist and can even act as a growing medium for some plants, such as jewel-like alpines, whose roots need moisture, but which grow best through a seemingly dry surface layer of loose stones.

tools • shovel • plank of wood • wooden mallet • trowel

materials • wooden edging • wooden stakes • suitable plants • coarse gravel

1 It is essential to ensure that the gravel is well bedded and retained by edges, or loose gravel will overflow onto the surrounding areas. Once you have decided where the gravel garden is to go, stake boards around the edge of the area to form a trough. Clear the soil of any perennial weeds. Place "molehills" of soil where you want your plants to be, then fill the trough with a thick layer of coarse gravel, being careful not to cover the "molehills" completely.

2 To ensure that your gravel is level, first use a board to sweep the surface, holding it at both ends and smoothing out any obvious

4

maintenance

Plants with sculptural shapes work well against a background of gravel, so you might want to work strictly with foliage plants. However, you could just as easily use your gravel to act as a neutral background for dramatic color effects in particular seasons. Helianthemums provide a wide range of dramatic red tones in summer – try 'Raspberry Ripple' or 'Wisley Pink.' The red autumn foliage of *Cerastostigma plumbaginoides* contrasts with the azure blooms it produces through late-summer and autumn, and wild thyme is good for winter color, particularly the variegated varieties such as 'Annie Hall' and 'Elfin.'

lumps. Then, with the board flat on the surface, either pound on it yourself, or hit it with a wooden mallet until the gravel is evenly distributed. Make sure that your molehills are completely surrounded.

3 Set the plants you have selected in the positions you have planned to see if they will give the effect you want, and then slide each plant carefully from its pot, inspecting the roots for weeds and pests, before positioning the plant in a hole big enough to accommodate the root ball. The plant should sit slightly high to leave room for the top layer of gravel. Backfill the hole, smoothing the surrounding soil.

4 Use the trowel to spread gravel over the exposed soil of the molehill. Repeat the process for each individual plant before covering the remainder of your plot with an even layer of fine gravel. Too deep a top layer will be difficult to keep flat if it is likely to be walked on, and very fine gravel is more likely to get displaced. If bare patches develop, simply replenish the affected areas with more gravel.

changes of level

Many nongardeners look in horror at a garden that is spread over a steep slope. Yet slopes offer a whole dimension that level gardens lack, often providing attractive views and the potential to create further vistas up or down. Any change in level tends to separate one part of a garden from another, which means that there is no need for the gardener to create artificial divisions.✲ Almost inevitably, these different areas will have a distinct character, and possibly their own

below **Brick steps provide an excellent solution where foot traffic is likely to be heavy at all times of year. Old bricks create a soft, weathered look.**

microclimates; for example, one area may have a better view and be more exposed. Part of the skill in developing an interesting garden on a slope lies in making the most of these different opportunities and problems.

making the best of a slope

Thinking back to the idea of dividing the garden into three zones,✲ the presence of a slope may mean that your middle zone, the bulk of the garden for most people, will have to be on the flattest piece of land, even if that is some distance from the house. Very steep banks almost automatically become outer zone areas. Many people try to maintain slopes as lawn grass, with all the mowing problems that this entails; it is much better either to let the grass grow and trim it every few months, and perhaps try to encourage a few wildflowers to grow, or to plant it with shrubs or ground cover plants. Many plants usually grown as climbers, such as clematis and honeysuckle *(Lonicera)*, can be grown as ground-covering trailers.

coping with changes in level

A crucial part of laying out a garden on a slope is working out how to manage the changes in level. Do you leave the slopes as they are or try to terrace them? What about access? Given that a garden of any size involves using a wheelbarrow, it would seem advisable to try to have a series of sloping paths up, or down, the garden, rather than having only steps. While paths need a fairly gentle gradient, which means that they might zigzag across the garden, steps are able to tackle much steeper gradients. It might be best to use steps for quick, easy access to the steeper parts of the garden and have another, slower "wheelbarrow-friendly" route.

far left **Many gardeners are shy of planting slopes, which is a shame because they offer exciting opportunities to enjoy plants from below and above. To keep maintenance low, choose reliable, weed-smothering varieties.**

left **Narrow steps, tightly surrounded by plants, create an atmosphere that encourages exploration. Many so-called rock garden plants will have the right creeping or cushion habit for this situation.**

terracing

Creating terraces is a time-honored way of turning slopes into strips of flat, easy-to-work land. They do involve an awful lot of work, though, not just in building the retaining walls for the soil, but in a great deal of earth-moving too. Since making a terrace involves digging into the slope, you may find that on thin soils you actually do not have enough

soil to make it possible or worthwhile. Really durable terracing involves stone walls, but these require a lot of time and muscle power to do on any scale. Wooden post-and-rail systems, where posts are driven into the ground with rails nailed horizontally to them, are the next best thing, and last many years if the wood is well treated with preservative.

 RELATED PAGES

34 boundaries and divisions

40 what goes where

project: steps

Steps can make a useful and decorative feature in a sloping garden. The principles behind the construction of safe, easy-to-use steps remain the same, whether they are wide, flat and gracefully curving, or shallow, straight and steep.

tools • shovel • trowel • level • brush • string, stake and hammer for early calculations

materials • cement • sand • water • flat stones

1 Calculate how many steps you need to build: divide the height of the slope by the height of one riser (including the depth of the flat stone that will form the tread). To make steps a comfortable height, the width of the tread and the height of the riser should be in proportion – as a rule, the width of the tread (at the outside edge if a curving step) plus double the height of the riser should measure about 26in. The treads should be deep enough for a secure footing, some 12in from front to back. Drive a stake into the ground at the foot of the bank and run a string horizontally from the bank to the stake. Measure from that point to the ground to give you the height of the bank. Dig the steps out of the bank and then mix your concrete.

4

choice of materials

Linking different parts of the garden both physically and visually, steps are an important structural element of any design. Intelligent planting – or strategically placed pots for instant effect – will link the steps to the rest of the garden. To be of practical benefit, however, your steps should be sited with convenience as well as visual effect in mind. It is easy to choose something that will harmonize with the rest of your garden because steps can be constructed from a wide variety of materials. Set on a concrete base, paving stones, loose gravel bounded by railroad ties, bricks set in patterns, flagstones, panels of decking – even sawn logs – all make good, solid steps, so choose materials to suit both your garden and your budget.

Using a shovel, mix six parts sand and one cement powder by volume in a heap, then make a hole in the top and pour water into it, little by little. Using a vertical cutting action, work the mixture until it is wet but will still stand in peaks.

2 Lay a good base of cement and start by building the first riser. When it is solid, backfill with stones, using a trowel to lay the cement mixture as mortar between each layer.

3 Even if the edges of the steps are left jagged, the top layer of stones must be level, with the tops of the stones aligned – uneven steps are unsafe. Once you have laid the tread of your first step, you can start with the riser of the next.

4 When you have finished, smooth any exposed cement mortar with a trowel, and brush the surfaces clean.

vital services

power supply

Electricity may be necessary in the garden, either to run a propagator or heater in the greenhouse or to power fountains or lighting. Since water and electricity are a notoriously dangerous mixture, it is imperative that the work is carried out by a qualified electrician.

water supply

A source of water is vital in the garden, especially if you intend to grow vegetables, or plants in containers, and you may find it worth the expense of laying a pipe to an easily accessed point. Modern plastic piping is easy to lay and very cheap. It is advisable to install a cut-off tap where the pipe is connected to the main supply; garden taps and pipes are prone to damage and leaks, and it should be possible to isolate them to prevent loss of water from the rest of the system.

seep hoses

As an alternative to watering by hand, you might consider a permanent irrigation system. A more sensitive ecological approach to gardening means that many gardeners who live in areas of low rainfall now choose plants to suit their site, rather than adapting their site to suit the plants. If irrigation is vital however, you may want to consider a seep hose. This is a system of perforated hosepipe laid at ground level or just below. Water seeps from the small holes and is delivered directly to the roots of the plants, resulting in minimum loss of water through evaporation.

Cables should be routed away from areas of regular cultivation and encased in steel tubing. Use a circuit breaker on any power line, and either connect cables to interior sockets or ensure exterior sockets are waterproof. For future reference, make a map of any outdoor cables when they are installed.

notebook
developing a framework

This chapter has explored the elements that make up the backbone of your garden. Permanent structures and features need careful thought if the rest of the garden is to be successful. The following pages provide space to plan and sketch specific elements of your garden in more detail.

plan a specific area

Plan a specific part of your garden here; maybe part of the inner zone such as a children's play area, a middle zone space such as an area of lawn surrounded by features and planting or an outer zone space such as a utility area or work space.

site survey

site measurements:

existing features:

existing planting:

action plan

tools required:

materials required:

planting required:

address book:

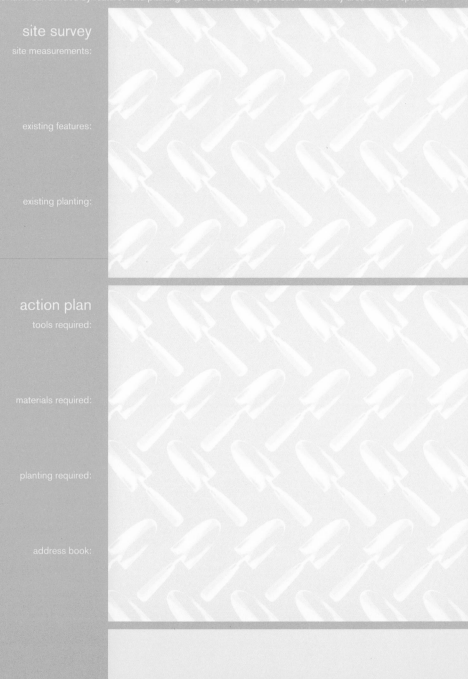

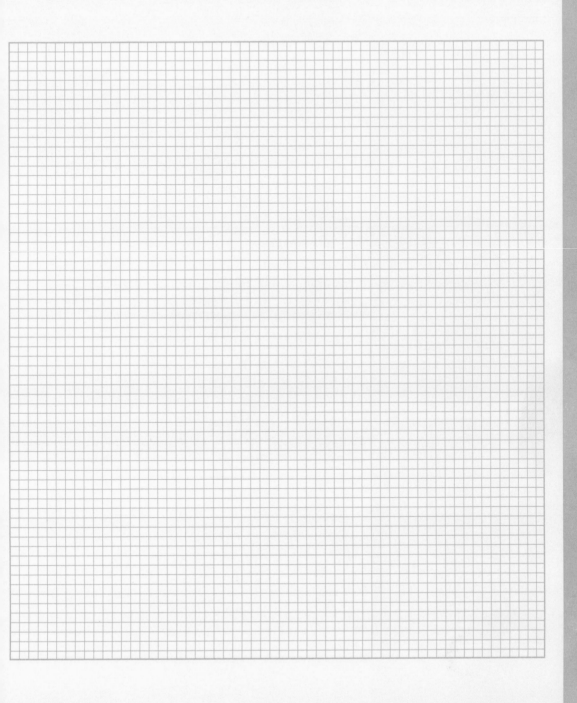

plan your garden surfaces

Use this space to plan the surfaces, either hard or soft, in your garden. You might want to plan walls or floors, a patio or area of decking, a gravel garden or an area of ornamental ground-cover planting.

site survey

site measurements:

existing features:

existing planting:

action plan

tools required:

materials required:

planting required:

address book:

plan your garden's changes of level

Focusing on the areas of your garden where the level changes, plan how you will deal with them, whether you want steps, a grassy bank or terracing, or to cut a turf seat into them.

site survey

site measurements:

existing features:

existing planting:

action plan

tools required:

materials required:

planting required:

address book:

features
and furniture

A garden without furniture or ornament can be a dull place. Imaginative choice of ornament will enhance your garden immensely, and if you get it right, practical features can be ornaments in their own right as well as being useful.

water

Water can transform a garden, not just because it adds another element but also because it automatically involves others – still water reflects the sky, bringing it to earth, while fountains and waterfalls introduce motion. Waterside and aquatic vegetation is often dramatically different from that of dry land, producing an exciting contrast. Water is often a focal point for a garden,* simply because it seems to always attract attention. Seating areas are often placed next to a pond for this reason.

below **Reflecting the sky is a magical part of water in gardens. This informally shaped pool is surrounded by a variety of low-growing perennial flowering plants, helping to create a relaxed, rural atmosphere.**

Because they are geometrical, our imaginations accept the concept of their being there at all. An informal pond, one with curving edges, only looks right in situations where it is conceivable that there could be a pond – in the country or large gardens, in dips and hollows. An informal pond on a slope, no matter how wild the surrounding garden, never looks right.

plants and wildlife

Formal ponds often have a few waterlilies and a limited amount of waterside vegetation; informal ones need to have much more in order to look as natural as possible. The great thing about waterside plants is how rapidly they grow, with their roots in moisture all through even the driest summers. Many look big and lush, with dramatically shaped leaves. Wildlife also establishes quickly in water; frogs, tadpoles and a variety of insects often appear with astonishing speed.* Indeed, the garden pond has become an important refuge for nature in built-up areas, and for many people this is the primary reason for building one.

ponds

The simplest water feature is a pond, of which there are two kinds: formal and informal. Formal ponds, with straight edges, look best in urban settings and small gardens, or indeed anywhere where it is unlikely that nature would put water.

moving water

Features that include moving water usually involve electricity. This entails digging trenches for cables, and the installation and concealing of equipment. Always employ the services of a qualified electrician when installing electricity in the garden. Recent developments in solar-power technology,

left Even the tiniest of gardens can have a pond. This old sink provides a cheap and effective object of interest in the garden and is home to several miniature water plants.

however, mean that it is now possible to run small moving features without laying cables, and with a lower and thus safer current. Fountains are popular in formal ponds; waterfalls are often included in informal ones. There is no reason why they should be so restricted – falling water can be used very effectively in urban settings that are dramatically different than the conventional rocky hillside.

small water features

If you have a tiny garden, you should not feel that you're excluded from water-gardening; it's possible to make a pond from an old barrel and grow a miniature waterlily. A range of small-scale water features is now easily available – some generate patterns in concrete basins with a soothing background sound that helps to drown out traffic noise,

left A Japanese-style fountain generates a cooling sound that helps to drown out intrusive noises such as traffic. The surrounding mosses and ivy (Hedera) enjoy cool, moist conditions in shade.

while others bubble water up and over mounds of pebbles. Not only do these water features fit into small spaces, but most of them are also completely safe for small children to be around.

 RELATED PAGES

98 plan your water feature
96 features for wildlife

project: fountain

It is easy to install a fountain if you use a kit, and there are now an increasing number available in garden centers and home centers. We used ceramic sculptures of sea urchins here, but you could just as easily use stones drilled with holes.

tools • spade

materials • water fountain kit • decorative outlets, if desired, such as sea urchins or millstones • pebbles • stones

1 Dig a deep hole big enough to accommodate the water tank so that its top is flush with the ground. Place the water circulation pump in the bottom of the tank and connect the electricity supply.
   Next fit together the water pipes so that they correspond with the number of sculptures you intend to use and their positions.

2 Push the water nozzle through the hole in the lid and then put the lid on the tank. Small drainage holes in the lid allow the water to circulate, but prevent stones or other debris from falling through and clogging the pump.

4

3 Raise your sculptures, so that there is enough room underneath for the water pipes; placing each one on a couple of bricks should be enough. Position the sculptures one by one, and test the flow from each nozzle in turn, adjusting the flow until you achieve the desired effect. For these sculptures, the water is adjusted to just bubble gently through the holes. You may prefer a stronger, higher jet of water depending on the sculptures you use and the positioning of your fountain.

4 Position the stones around the sculpture carefully to avoid damaging the water pipes. Be sure to select a style of fountain that suits your garden. Without our urchin sculptures, you would create the effect of a bubbling spring; simply by adding a nozzle, the water would be forced to rise with more power, creating a classic jet fountain. When adjusting the height of a water jet, remember that the height of the water spout should not exceed the radius of the basin in which it is placed, or the water will be blown in the wind and you will lose water from the tank.

do it differently

You only need to buy the pump equipment in order to build a simple fountain like this. If you sink a tub or half of a barrel into a hole in the ground, and place the pump on a brick at the bottom, you can support the decorative pebbles on wire mesh laid across the top of the tank. Think about whether pebbles are the correct texture for your site. The sound of water will enhance any garden, and you can also substitute various materials to create different sound effects: mossy stones absorb sound, while metal or pottery will give a higher-pitched, tinkling effect. Of course, you could vary the material according to your mood.

the vertical dimension

scrambling habit adds a touch of romance. Self-clinging climbers like ivies *(Hedera)* and Virginia creeper *(Parthenocissus quinquefolia)* are very useful for covering walls; this helps to insulate houses from extremes of heat and cold, and to protect the surface of any rendering. Other climbers, including most flowering climbers, need something they can curl a tendril around or twine through. This need may be satisfied by something unobtrusive such as wires stretched tightly between firmly fixed attachments, or by something that becomes an ornamental feature in its own right. A trellis, attached to a bare wall, fills up space before climbers have covered it, and also in the winter when the plants may have lost their leaves. It can be painted to contrast with the color of the wall or the plant. Climbers can also be grown up dead trees, or even mature live trees, if carefully matched to their support.

above Gardeners with limited space need to be imaginative. The space down the side of a house can often be a dark and depressing area, but here it has been transformed by clever use of climbers and wall-trained shrubs.

Gardens do not just happen on level ground. Any vertical surface is a potential place to grow a climber, which is good news for those who have small urban gardens with more wall or fence area than flat ground. Any garden benefits from the introduction of climbing plants, but choosing a climber of the appropriate size is vital, however, since some can get very big very quickly. "Wall shrubs" are freestanding shrubs grown as if they were climbers, trained to grow tightly against walls or fences, either by being tied to wires or trellises or by being pruned to shape. Many are slightly tender, best grown against a sunny wall in cooler climates.

Climbers appeal for several reasons; they grow rapidly, creating a sense of maturity in young gardens, and their

walls and fences

If you have a warm, sunny wall, consider wall shrubs such as ceanothus and myrtle *(Myrtus communis)* that will relish the warmth as well as tolerate the poor soil conditions that often prevail in this situation. Choosing plants for walls that receive little sun, or that experience strong, cold winds, needs particular care, since few climbers relish shade. Variegated ivies, and the yellow *Clematis orientalis* and *C. tangutica*, are usually the best sources of color. Exposed sites need plants that are reliably hardy.

freestanding supports

These can be used as supports for climbers to create eye-catching vertical features. Archways allow you to get up close and smell fragrant plants like roses, but when you choose the climber remember that you will need to be able to walk through without being ensnared when it is fully grown. Archways develop a path from one part of the garden to another. When planning your garden ✳ think of archways and arbors as interior design features, acting as doorways and corridors to different rooms of the garden.

Obelisks introduce height quickly in relatively formal gardens, and are especially effective when used as a centerpiece to a border or the "panels" of formal planting schemes, where shrubs would be unsuitable because of their bulk and sideways spread. Wigwams, or other similar arrangements of branches, are a more naturalistic possibility for the informal garden.

left **Raised beds lift the planting off ground level, while a climber-covered trellis and a wooden plant support both contribute to the feeling of height in this planting scheme.**

below **An arch of trees not only adds height to the garden, but also frames the view through to another area. Occasional clipping shapes the arch.**

Roses clambering up the house might sound romantic, especially in country areas, but bear in mind that they are the least easy climbers to train and require tying to supports. This may be a problem if it entails balancing on a ladder far above the ground.

If you want to cover a wall, fence or eyesore completely, make sure you select a climber that will grow big enough or is perhaps a little too big, and be prepared to keep cutting it back. Planting several will help too. If you want to keep some of the structure visible, if it is a nice old wall for example, buy smaller-growing plants, and consider how different flower and leaf colors will look against it. If the wall or fence is a backdrop for a border, you will need to bear the climbers in mind as part of the plan for the other planting.

✳ **RELATED PAGES**

20 planning your garden

directory: plant supports

wooden trellis

supporting climbers
Few climbers can manage to climb by themselves – ivy *(Hedera* sp.*)* and virginia creepers *(Parthenocissus* sp.*)* have suckers which enable them to self-cling to most surfaces, but others need something to wind around. The easiest and most unobtrusive way to do this on walls is to use wires, firmly fixed by small metal hooks called "vine-eyes." Constructions of wood or metal are commonly used on walls as well and can become a decorative feature in their own right.

Climbers do not have to be restricted to walls; it is now common practice to use a variety of free-standing supports, which allow you to use climbers much more widely in a whole range of garden situations. These can be multifunctional, such as archways, or decorative in themselves, such as obelisks.

practicalities
Climbing plants use a variety of mechanisms to move up supports. Many, such as honeysuckles *(Lonicera* sp.*)*, twine, which allows them to hang on to both thick and thin supports, while others, notably clematis, use flexible leaf stems. Some have highly specialized tendrils, like the passion flowers *(Passiflora* sp.*)*, the latter needing quite thin supports to hang on to. Roses use their thorns in nature, and in cultivation need some help in climbing, such as having their young growth bent around the supports or being tied in with twine.

It is important that the size of the support is matched with that of the climber – too large and there will be masses of growth at the top, too small and there will be a lot of bare support. Climbers can be heavy when fully grown too, so supports should be securely made.

The materials used for supports should be relatively maintenance-free, as they will inevitably weather, and getting access to them to repaint or repair through a mass of growth is not going to be easy.

natural log support

bamboo poles

metal pergola

popular for self-standing supports but will only take the weight of comparatively light plants. For this reason they are favored for use in containers or with annuals such as sweet peas.

metal Metal supports are strong and durable, but unless you have skills and equipment, they will need to be made to order by an appropriate craftsperson. The strength of metal makes it particularly suitable for supporting large climbers on high walls, or for substantial garden features such as arbors. As a material, it lends itself to innovative and contemporary design, with the incorporation of industrial materials such as heavy-duty meshes often making the construction of such pieces economic.

wood and other natural materials

Wood is the easiest and most versatile material with which to make plant supports. Lattice, easily and relatively cheaply purchased at any garden center, can be sawn to fit any space; archways and freestanding supports are also simple to make with a minimum of skill and some basic tools. The more ambitious may wish to try their hand at a freestanding trellis, or an archway or arbor.

Sawn timber needs some sort of protection from the weather if it is not to decay quickly – either a coating of paint over a layer of primer, or treatment with a (plant-friendly) preservative. Painted or stained wood can be an effective garden ornament by itself, and colors can be chosen to match flowers or foliage.

Uncut lumber can be used to make more rustic-style supports and has the advantage that its uncut surfaces resist decay well and so do not need treatment with preservative.

Bamboo poles and thin rods of flexible woods like willow or hazel are

metal column

garden ornament

right **This spiral is a dramatic but relatively low-key addition to a garden. It takes up very little space and is effectively transparent. In small gardens it is important that sculptures do not dominate.**

Garden ornament can be exciting and contemporary, innovative and fun – despite the fact that the words may conjure up visions of garden gnomes, pseudoclassical urns or statues of seminaked nymphs. It is usually intended to be permanent, and in the context of a garden, where everything growing is in a state of constant flux, this is a great advantage. In bare winter months, ornament may be the garden's chief interest.

above **A small artistic feature like a suspended stained glass picture can transform an otherwise dull corner. Blue is a particularly attractive color in the garden throughout the year.**

using ornament

Through most of garden history, ornament has tended to occupy center stage, with planting often simply a backdrop. The harder lines and often distinctive colors of an ornament mean that it stands out among plants, making it particularly useful for creating a focal point. Modern gardens, however, are more likely to integrate ornament and planting, matching the color of the ornament with flowers and foliage, or using the two in concert, for example by growing ivy (Hedera) next to stonework, evoking a ruined building.

creating ambience

Ornament is a vital part of developing a particular ambience in a garden; abstract sculptures connote modernism, colorful mosaics evoke the Mediterranean. To be really successful there must be consistency,

however; the appearance of a Grecian column in between bamboo and a Japanese lantern will not help develop an oriental theme. There is room for eclecticism, the gathering together of different cultural artifacts, but it needs to be done well to work, with something, such as color or planting, that creates a unity of style.✳

objets trouvés

Garden ornament can be frighteningly expensive. But the use of found objects – objets trouvés – is one of the most enjoyable and inexpensive ways of making garden ornaments. Found objects can be enjoyed for what they are, given center stage like an expensive statue, or left lying around casually to add to a particular mood.

Using natural objects seems an obvious thing to do in a garden, matching stone and wood with plants, and yet it also lends quite a contemporary feel. Stones and pebbles, especially, may be selected to contrast with

the shapes of particular plants or to evoke the mood of a particular environment. Wood usually looks good with stone, and gnarled stumps and driftwood, carved by nature into richly tangled shapes, are often very effective. Stumps and pieces of partially decayed wood used around shade-loving plants help to create the feeling of a forest, while pebbles and driftwood recreate the beach. Using such materials in rural gardens may be unnecessary, but in urban settings they can be employed to create a sense of the garden being somewhere else, if desired.

Using artificial materials can be equally effective, however: a vast range of items discarded by others as trash can be utilized by the imaginative gardener. Some can be put to a practical purpose – cable reels, for example, can be made into tables and chairs – while others serve only an ornamental function. For it to be effective, careful display is important if something that may seem like a piece of rubbish is to appear decorative. The sculptural qualities of old machinery, for example, may be better appreciated if it is placed on a pedestal of some kind. A wide range of discarded items are commonly used as containers. An old boat full of flowers is a familiar idea, but oil drums and other industrial containers often make first-rate planters if suitably painted. Small items can be combined to create a whole greater than the sum of the parts: using broken glass, tiles and pottery to make a mosaic is a well-established technique, but with a little imagination, you will also be able to take old mechanical bits and pieces, such as hinges, handles, bolts and springs, and turn them into sculptures, figurative or abstract.

practicalities

You can usually transform manufactured *objets trouvés* by giving them a quick coat of paint, which turns them from rubbish into an art object. Unless you apply this properly, however, your paint is likely to come off as quickly as it went on when you expose it to the elements. It is essential to make sure you use an appropriate primer; this will bond the paint securely.

above ***Objets trouvés*** **cost nothing and can be among the most effective garden ornaments; and if you tire of them, they can be cast aside. Great satisfaction can be found in arranging and re-arranging such finds.**

✳ **RELATED PAGES**

10 garden styles

directory: containers

When selecting containers, it is worth thinking ahead to how you will get the plant out when it needs to be potted or disposed of. Traditional pots have sloping sides for the very good reason that they make it easier to remove the plants, although this is often still difficult. It is practically impossible to get a live plant out of a straight-sided pot – let alone an incurving container – without major damage, either to plant or pot.

terracotta This is the traditional, and still favorite, material for containers, its warm earthy tones complementing both flowers and foliage. It is porous, which means that plants do dry out more quickly than in other types of container, but this has the effect of helping to cool the roots in warm weather. Terracotta varies tremendously in price and quality. The big question is whether or not it is frostproof, and the cheaper containers usually are not. Frostproof terracotta is fired to a higher temperature and is coarser in texture; if it is physically hard and made in a country which experiences cold winters, then it probably is going to survive the winter without shattering. Terracotta that is not frostproof can be made so by painting with varnish, which will render it impermeable to water.

glazed ceramics Glazing terracotta also makes it frostproof, but only if the inside is glazed too. Glaze adds color and thus the potential of choosing glazes that reflect or contrast with certain flower colors for example, or using the containers to develop a color theme in the garden.

Though not cheap, some of the most interesting containers now being made are those glazed pottery products produced by a number of innovative craftspeople. Often inspired by Far Eastern or African designs, they can be works of art in their own right.

wood and wicker Containers made of wood and wicker have the advantage of being relatively light and portable when empty. Many different

styles are available, from formal Versailles tubs to painted half barrels, to rustic wicker baskets. Hardwood is the more durable choice for wooden containers, and if softwood is used, you should either buy pressure-treated lumber or paint it with preservative once a year. All of them can be painted either to complement the plants grown in them or to continue a color theme present in other garden elements.

cement and artificial stone Like plastic, these have a somewhat downmarket image, largely because they are used to create poor imitations of other products, such as Grecian urns and classical nymphs, all too often with a highly visible seam where they have been taken out of the mold. When used for simple and unpretentious containers though, the material can be highly effective. It is certainly durable, and its weight can even be an advantage, when using top-heavy plants for example.

Imitation stone ornaments can be transformed by a coat of masonry paint, or even better, by painting them lots of different colors, which in fact is what the ancient Greeks did anyway.

plastic and fiberglass
Plastic pots are light, a major consideration for anyone who has to lug around large ceramic pots. Traditionally, though, they have lacked charm, or even begun to disintegrate after a few years of exposure to sunlight. A new generation of plastic containers is changing the

galvanized container

image of this versatile material, by imitating traditional materials so well that a close look is needed to ascertain what they are made from.

Fiberglass is a more rigid material, which has found application in the manufacture of garden containers, perhaps the most spectacular to date being some remarkably lifelike imitations of traditional lead containers.

metal and galvanized containers
Metal containers have recently become popular – galvanized buckets and pots in particular. Their clean lines and appearance enhance contemporary environments, and they are probably here to stay, although continued use will result in the coating

being damaged, leading to rusting. The use of copper or lead containers is limited to those able to afford them, although very good fiberglass imitations are now available. The green patina of copper is remarkable, but can be readily imitated using paint.

found objects
Anything that can contain earth may be used for growing plants in, although containers that have been used to transport toxic chemicals should be avoided. Holes in the bottom are essential to allow for drainage, but these are usually easy to make.

A disadvantage of some found containers is their appearance, but this can usually be improved by a coat of paint or by covering them in some way, by wrapping a barrel in burlap for example.

fiberglass pot

wicker wall basket

project: painted pots

Painting containers is an ideal way to liven up bland mass-produced pots: it is easy, inexpensive, and the results can be stunning. There are a variety of methods from which to choose, depending on the effect you want to achieve.

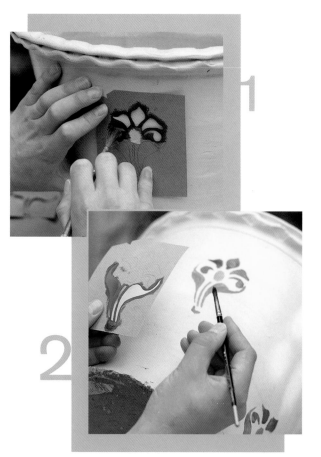

For the stencilled pot:
tools • craft knife • artist's brush
materials • plastic stencil film • tracing paper • acrylic paints

For the amphora:
tools • large paintbrush • protective eye goggles
materials • limewash • latex paint

For the striped pot:
tools • masking tape • artist's brush
materials • solvent-based paint

1 Stencils offer the opportunity to create complex and sophisticated patterns. To make your stencil, first choose a simple shape, such as the flower motif shown here. Trace the shape onto tracing paper and transfer to plastic film. For this stencil you will need three pieces of plastic stencil film for the three colors used.

4

preparation and finishing

Surface preparation and waterproofing are essential if your work is to be long-lasting. Porous terracotta should be sealed with a stabilizer and appropriate primers used on other materials to ensure even adhesion of paint. A layer of exterior clear varnish over the finished work will ensure protection from the weather. Treat terracotta in this way, varnished inside as well as out, and it will then be frostproof.

Make a notch in the same place in the corner of each one, and a corresponding pencil mark on the pot, to ensure correct positioning of each successive stencil.

2 Allow each color to dry thoroughly before applying the next. After the final stencil a little touching up by hand may be necessary.

3 Limewashing is an ideal way to create a rough, antique look on porous terracotta. Mix latex paint with limewash, bearing in mind that it will dry a few shades lighter, and brush it roughly onto the pot using a large brush. Limewash is caustic, so rubber gloves are advisable and eye protection is vital.

4 To paint stripes on pots, apply two strips of masking tape for each stripe. Paint between the lines carefully to avoid getting paint under the tape and allow the paint to dry thoroughly before removing the tape. This pot was painted using a solvent-based paint, but water-based emulsion or acrylic paints are suitable alternatives.

seating

Seating plays a crucial role in our enjoyment of a garden. Even the most fanatical gardener will want at some stage to sit down, relax and admire their work, and even if they do not, they will have friends and family who will. Seating is central to two of the most important functions of the garden – relaxation and entertaining.

seats for relaxing

For most people who garden, it is the element of relaxation that is perhaps most important. A garden is somewhere in which

below This striking carved bench still has the feel and texture of something natural, even primitive, earning itself a place in a shaded jungly garden.

to escape, to unwind, and to enjoy nature and the results of all your hard work. A seat is the key place to experience this, either alone or with company. You can not only appreciate the garden from the seat, but perhaps views out of the garden as well.

Seats may be outward- or inward-looking, the former being orientated to a vista over the entire garden or views beyond, whereas the latter are more likely to be in a secluded place, a shell in which you may hide from the outside world. Arbors, gazebos and secret gardens fulfill this function in many Western gardens; in Japan, there is a tradition of teahouse gardens, which are secluded, meditative places.✱

The bench has become the standard piece of furniture from which to soak up the calming qualities of garden and landscape. While there are some good and imaginative designs available, most are traditional, either wooden or (imitation) cast iron, the latter usually inspired by Victorian designs. Benches are sometimes built into garden features — for example, slate slabs as part of a stone structure such as a wall, or a turf seat✱ dug into the earth itself.

seats for entertaining

Social seating demands more flexibility than fixed seats can offer. Entertaining usually involves a table, seats and perhaps a place to barbecue as well. Plenty of space is needed to fit all this in, as well as proximity to the house if cooking is likely to be

complicated or dinner parties frequent. Seats should complement the scene, which may rule out the very cheap, plastic seats that are readily available. If your budget is tight, consider using backless benches which seat two to three people at a table, or sawn-off widths of tree trunk as stools. If you have access to some good slabs of stone or planks of wood, you can easily improvise a rough-and-ready seat by propping them on sawn-off tree trunks or similarly shaped large stones, just as long as the structure is stable. Tables should perhaps be the priority in the budget, being more difficult to improvise.

attractive surroundings

Whatever the nature of the seating arrangements, their immediate surroundings are of crucial importance to their enjoyment, all the more if the seat is of the intimate or contemplative kind. Fragrant climbers are irresistibly romantic, but might need something else at ground level for when the climbers stop flowering. Plantings of quiet colors, and simple and elegant shapes, are necessary around a seat for meditation, while the attraction of water almost demands that a pond or other water feature is accompanied by a seat.

above **Contemporary gardens need striking furniture. This wave-backed seat enables hosts and guests to enjoy the sunset over a spectacular view.**

 RELATED PAGES

12 developing a style

56 turf seat

directory: seating

Materials are a major factor when choosing seating, because those which fail to suit their surroundings can have a major impact on the rest of the garden. Appearance and cost are only part of the equation though, weight and durability being other considerations.

wood Probably still the most commonly used seating material, wood offers versatility, and when unpainted, has a natural surface that is appropriate to practically any kind of garden. Rustic seats made from deliberately crude wood fit into country gardens but look out of place in more formal surroundings. They are fun to make and cost little.

Furniture made from softwoods is relatively cheap and lightweight but is likely to decay much more quickly than

wooden bench

that made from hardwoods. It needs to be well protected with preservative, which should be reapplied every few years, well before the season when it is due to be used, to allow time for the preservative to dry out and lose some of its distinctive smell. Painting with a protective finish makes for greater durability, as well as being attractive, enabling you to fit seating into a garden color scheme.

Most good-quality seats are made from hardwoods such as teak, which are potentially very long-lasting. They are generally preserved through the use of oils, such as teak oil, which should be applied every winter. Most hardwoods used these days come from managed plantations rather than from virgin rainforest, but it is advisable to check the origin of the materials used.

Benches are the most popular type of wooden seating and are regarded as essential by many. A practical variant, seen surprisingly little, is the version that has two handles at one end and a wheel at the other, allowing it to be easily wheeled out of the way when mowing the grass or to follow or avoid the sun.

Adirondack seats or loungers are the classic American garden seating, now available in other countries. They are very comfortable, but heavy.

stone The natural color and variation of stone such as granite, slate or marble makes it an attractive option for garden seating with styles ranging from simple rustic boulders to ornately carved benches. It is heavy and extremely durable, so care is needed when choosing and placing stone

stone bench

seating. Such seating needs little or no maintenance.

metal The Victorian era saw the rise of metal garden furniture, much of it made from cast iron, detailed with highly ornate and distinctive patterns. Such furniture is essential to create a period look, complementing Victorian-style conservatories and nineteenth-

painted wrought iron

century architecture. Some modern furniture is made with traditional materials and designs, while some uses metals such as wrought iron to create other, usually more lightweight and elegant designs.

Weight is the main disadvantage of metal furniture, especially of cast iron, although recent years have seen the use of lighter materials such as steel mesh, which can be very attractive. Corrosion is a more long-term problem, and older pieces may need professional restoration. Metal furniture should be inspected regularly for signs of damage to the protective paintwork, which should be touched up as soon as possible. Brush off the rust and apply an antirust paint and then a metal primer, before adding further layers.

plastic Plastic furniture is remarkably cheap, and usually looks it. Paying a little more though can get you some better-quality pieces, although these tend to be imitations of other materials, rather than the contemporary design that this modern material is more suited to. Cheap plastic furniture can be improved with paint, but the surface needs to be well sanded before the paint has any chance of sticking.

built-in seating A favorite place in the garden can have a seat built into it; this is a durable, and potentially inexpensive, option. The basic shape may be easily dug into a slope, with turves of lawn grass, slabs of slate or bricks used to line the seat and back. Wooden built-in seating is a traditional

plastic seating

option, perhaps built around a tree trunk, although don't forget that you should leave room for the trunk to grow to maturity.

built-in seating

entertaining

very different eyes from when you are planning areas for flowers or vegetables or for quiet relaxation. On what scale are you likely to entertain? The requirements for small groups of people, in informal gatherings, differ greatly from those of more formal functions that command a high number of guests, such as large birthday or wedding parties. Whatever your ambitions, however, you will always want to create a sense of awe and admiration in your visitors when they experience your garden layout and planting.

small gatherings

If you want to use your garden to entertain small groups of people, whether for informal lunches or barbecues, or for more formal alfresco cocktail parties or dining, the terrace or patio is perhaps the most important area. It is important that it is located in a convenient place and offers good views, either into the rest of the garden or over the surrounding townscape or countryside. The immediate vicinity of such an area needs to be stimulating, perhaps with some

above **Alfresco dinner parties require plenty of space around the table, with room for adding more tables if necessary. The lighting makes it possible to appreciate the garden on such occasions.**

Gardens for entertaining need to supply both space for practical purposes and sources of interest and enjoyment for visitors.✷ Those who do a lot of entertaining usually want to impress their guests with the beauty of their garden at the same time as providing a pleasant and comfortable setting for eating, drinking and talking. Making an area for entertaining involves looking at your site with

plants, planting combinations, a fountain or ornament that is unusual enough to spark off conversations. Anything that gets people talking to each other is a boon for the social gardener.

large parties

Large parties demand space for guests to wander in, to talk and maybe even to dance. A decent-sized area of lawn near the patio, terrace or other focal point is essential, but one too large may create a lack of intimacy. Just as important are more secluded areas where guests may wander off from the crowd, whether to discuss business deals in private or for more social pursuits. Victorian novels often feature shrubberies as the setting for romantic trysts during social functions. The modern garden needs similar enclosed spaces to which people can escape in order to feel private, and yet still be within easy reach of the main gathering, in case anything should demand their attention.

inspirational planting

There is nothing like unusual or exotic planting to stimulate discussion. Careful attention to planting key areas that everyone will have to pass – the front of the house or an area seen first by guests – is vital, as well as more social areas. Scented climbers trained to grow up panels of lattice adjacent to a patio or terrace will make a welcoming impression, while half-hardy exotics such as palms and daturas, with their huge, night-

fragrant trumpets, will create the right sort of environment for a balmy summer evening. Container plantings✳ are especially useful for social settings, as they can be moved around to make space for various activities or be arranged into a group to create an attractive focal point wherever one is needed.

above **In a large garden, space for entertaining can be easily defined simply by placing garden tables and chairs in a welcoming arrangement before your guests arrive.**

left **Ideal dining places outside should be in the evening sun for as long as possible and be near a door that allows easy access to the kitchen.**

✳ **RELATED PAGES**

9 integrated gardens
146 containers

project: barbecue

Many people consider a barbecue to be an essential part of summer entertaining. While it is possible to build a temporary one, it only takes confidence and a little effort to construct a permanent feature that will give you pleasure for years.

3

1

2

tools • trowel • long level • wooden mallet • masonry chisel

materials • charcoal tray • cooking grill • 12 metal supports • bricks • sand • cement • shelf

1 First, decide where to situate your barbecue. It should not be too close to walls, fences or trees where it could be a fire hazard. You may also want to position it so that you do not have your back to guests while cooking. A solid foundation is needed so that it will be stable.

Start by laying the first layer of bricks onto the ground. To check the size of the cooking area, lay the cooking grill on the ground as well, and place the bricks around it. Use the level to check that the first brick layer is level. Any bricks that are slightly higher or lower than others can be built up underneath with a larger amount of concrete.

4

materials

Durable materials are important for the construction of barbecues, so brick and stone, or reconstituted stone, are the obvious choices. Reclaimed brick, like that used here, can be bought relatively inexpensively and looks extremely effective. New bricks, although they will weather in time, look stark in most gardens and are probably only suitable in the gardens of very modern houses. Cooking grills and charcoal trays can either be purchased in kit form or commissioned to your own specifications from a blacksmith or welder. Those which are supplied in kit form normally contain metal supporting tabs as well; otherwise these are easily purchased from a good hardware store. Stainless steel is the best option for cooking grills; although it is more expensive than other materials, it is more durable and easy to clean.

2 Mix the concrete following the instructions on page 63. Lay the first layer of bricks and then start to build up the sides, starting with the corners. This makes it is easier to check that both the walls are vertical as you go. Keep checking this, and that the corners align horizontally with each other.

3 Use a masonry chisel and a wooden mallet to cut bricks for the ends where necessary.

4 Our barbecue has three sets of four metal supports: one set for the charcoal tray, one for the lower cooking position and one for the higher. Insert the metal supports in between the layers as you go, making sure that they are absolutely level and are protruding far enough to provide sufficient support. The shelf is inserted in the same way.

features for wildlife

Natural homes for wildlife have been drastically reduced by habitat destruction, much of it carried out to create homes and gardens for us. Gardeners can do a great deal for conservation by providing places where wild animals can feel safe to feed, roost and breed, as well as adding interest to the garden.

Not being overly neat is the best way to start catering for wildlife. Dead flower stems left standing over the winter provide birds and small mammals with food; heaps of old logs provide hibernating places for small mammals and food for insects; and patches of nettles are a source of food for butterfly larvae. Needless to say, the absolute minimum use of chemicals – insecticides especially – is vital for wildlife gardening. Since gardens naturally harbor a wide range of insects that eat pests (such as ladybugs which feed on aphids), problems will often sort themselves out in time anyway.

above **Doves make an attractive addition to a garden. Here wild and domestic animal life is catered for by a pond and dense and varied planting.**

planting

Native plant species tend to support a richer insect fauna than that of nonnative plants, and more insects means more food for birds. A combination of short and long grass, perennials, shrubs, climbers and trees will provide the maximum amount of roosting and nesting places. If butterflies and moths are a particular interest, find out what the food plants for the species likely to be found in your area are; larvae and adults usually feed on different species, the adults being less discriminating, with late-summer flowers like buddleja attracting large numbers.

ponds

Wildlife is able to make most use of a pond if the water is surrounded by a mixture of grass sloping down to the edge and waterside vegetation, with a minimum of sharp drops down to the water. In the water itself, a gradient from muddy marginal planting to the bottom along a sloping floor provides water creatures with the best range of options. Some shade over the pond for part of the day, or alternatively waterlilies, helps to keep fish and others cool in summer.

birdhouses and feeders

These are not only a good way of caring for wildlife, but also provide an opportunity to observe birds at fairly close quarters. Birdhouses should be situated in a secluded spot and placed high up to prevent attacks by ground-based predators. While the commonly sold birdhouses cater for a large range of smaller species, there are specialized ones available for others. Bird feeders can be placed closer to the house, as birds will be much braver when food is scarce in winter.

notebook
features and furniture

This chapter has taken you through the options available when choosing features and furniture. So with the major elements of your garden planned, you can focus on planning more specific ones.

plan your water feature

site survey

site measurements:

existing features:

existing planting:

action plan

tools required:

materials required:

planting required:

address book:

plan your vertical elements

Use this space to sketch the design and position of vertical elements of your garden such as archways, arches, arbors, obelisks and ornamental plant supports.

site survey

site measurements:

existing features:

existing planting:

action plan

tools required:

materials required:

planting required:

address book:

plan your barbecue

site survey
site measurements:

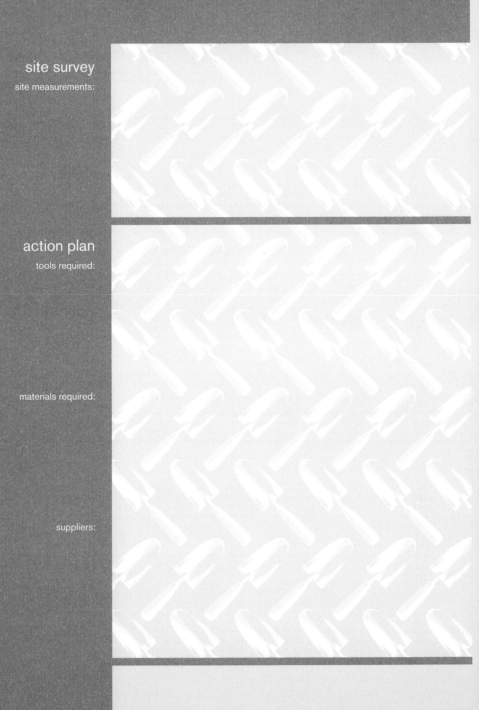

action plan
tools required:

materials required:

suppliers:

creative
planting

Putting plants together to create stunning planting schemes may seem like an impossible task for the beginner, but a little attention to the basics of combining plants soon takes the mystery out of the process.

plant types

A garden is nothing without plants.✱ They not only embellish the garden, but connect us to seasonal change and the beauties and realities of the natural world: fresh spring growth, summer lushness, rich autumn colors and dry winter stems.

trees

Trees are woody plants with (usually) one stem, or trunk. It may appear that there is little space for them in many gardens, yet there are varieties that do not take up that much room. Those sold for their flower (such as flowering cherries) tend to be on the small side, and there are many that have a narrow shape that makes them particularly suitable for smaller gardens. Trees may be planted for practical reasons: for shade, as windbreakers or for other screening purposes. Otherwise they are chosen for flower, foliage (often autumn color), fruit (which may be edible) or their shape. Given their size and permanence the most popular varieties, especially for small gardens, are those which can fulfill more than one of these purposes, for example those that flower, bear fruit and have an elegant shape.

above Trees for small gardens need to be chosen carefully, both for size and appeal. *Magnolia* x *soulangeana* is widely planted for its spectacular show of spring flowers and compact shape.

shrubs

Shrubs are woody plants with multiple stems. While flowers are the primary reason for choosing shrubs, it is their bulk and their ability to furnish and divide up space that are their most crucial characteristics. Unfortunately, many grow to be quite large, and since they are promoted heavily by garden centers, it is all too easy for a garden to be reduced to overgrown scrub after a few years. I advise caution in choosing shrubs, making sure to find out how large they will eventually become. As well as flowers, some have striking autumn berries, others attractive foliage. Few have good autumn colors, though, and very few have a particularly graceful natural shape, although some, such as the well-known and adaptable *Fatsia japonica,* have dramatic foliage.

climbers

We have already seen how useful climbers are in gardens where there are vertical surfaces to cover.✱ A unique characteristic of climbers, compared to shrubs and perennials, is how easily controllable their size is, because they will only go as far as their support will take them. Choice of an appropriately sized support for the variety of climber you choose is important.

dwarf shrubs

This category covers those shrubs, like heathers and lavenders, that form a low twiggy mat, useful for ground cover, often evergreen and, in many cases, tolerant of harsh conditions. They are most suitable for combining with perennials of similar size, making use of both their flowers and the attractive foliage and form of many.

perennials

These are the mainstay of the smaller garden, plants that have an annual cycle of growth, mostly dying back in winter, to regrow in spring. Whereas shrubs tend to flower in spring, most perennials (and virtually all the larger ones) flower in summer. They are particularly useful for the impatient, as they establish, and give pleasing results, so much more quickly than woody plants.

bulbs

Bulbs are perennials in packaged form, the perfect plants for quick results, and the back-bone of the spring garden. There are many good summer ones though, such as lilies. Most, but not all, flower reliably every year.

annuals and biennials

Annuals have a life cycle of one year, growing from seed, flowering, setting seed and dying within that time. They are grown from seed either where they are to flower (hardy annuals) or under cover first and only planted after the risk of late frosts is over (half-hardy annuals). The latter category includes many species that are really perennials, but are treated as annuals in cooler climates. The great thing about all annuals is the speed with which they develop and the freedom with which they flower throughout the summer. Biennials follow the same life cycle as annuals, but over two years instead of one, spending the first year developing growth and flowering and setting seed in the second year.

below **Bulbs are indispensable for springtime. Some, such as daffodils, are long-lived, flowering more profusely each year. Others, especially tulips, need annual replacing for best results.**

left **Perennials are the mainstay of the summer garden. Most are remarkably long-lived, with long flowering seasons. The opium poppies on the left are annuals but self-seed to bloom each year.**

✳ **RELATED PAGES**

162 plant selector
78 the vertical dimension

using a plant notebook

In my experience the best means of learning about plants is to visit gardens open to the public. Not only will you see a wide variety of plants, but you will see how they grow, in what kinds of conditions they do well, and how they combine with other plants. You may also see plants illustrated or written about in books and magazines, and find it useful to learn more about them in reference books,* to see how suitable they would be for your own garden.

In order to make the most of all this information you will need to record it in a form that can be easily accessed. A good garden notebook,* perhaps with a computer database if you begin to accumulate a lot of material, is as essential a tool as a spade.

names

Noting the Latin (scientific) names of plants is important as they are universally recognized (although frequently argued about by botanists). They comprise two or three parts: the first part (*Rosa* in *Rosa rugosa*) names the genus, which is a group of very similar plants, and the second the species. Any further names, usually in roman rather than italic type, are the names of specific varieties bred for garden use. Some of these will be selections of species chosen for their particular garden value, or they may be hybrids, the result of a cross between two varieties or species. The name of the hybrid is usually indicated in ordinary script following the genus, such as *Rosa* 'Iceberg.'

plant descriptions

These should note plant type, i.e., whether it is a tree, shrub, perennial, etc.; flower color and foliage interest; or whatever it was that attracted you to the plant in the first place. Size may be an important part of the description, but bear in mind that woody plants, such as trees, shrubs and most climbers, will often not be anything like their full size. The time of year the plants were seen may also be relevant.

The next stage after noting plants that you like is to note combinations. Particular flower-color juxtapositions may be striking, or the proximity of flowers with foliage, or it may be the way some spring bulbs are growing beneath flowering trees or shrubs.

growing conditions

Any good garden reference book will tell you the favored growing conditions of garden plants, yet this may often be supplemented, or perhaps contradicted, by your own observations. If a plant is growing particularly well, especially if it has obviously been growing there for many years, make a note of such factors as light and shade, whether it is in moist or dry soil, and whether it is growing close to trees or shrubs. If favorite plants are languishing, make a note of their growing conditions too. This kind of observation is especially important in gardens close to your own, since the reason the books may be wrong is that they may be written from the perspective of a different climate zone or soil type. There are also often exceptions to rules; for example it is common knowledge that rhododendrons cannot be grown on alkaline (lime-rich soils) but in fact some are more lime-tolerant than others.

talking to gardeners

Experienced gardeners in your area, or the owners or staff of gardens open to the public, are usually only too glad to pass on information. Asking about a plant in someone's garden will often be the key to learning about its essential requirements, including esoteric likes and dislikes that will never be found in books. It may also lead to the offer of a cutting or even a whole plant; an aristocratic garden owner that I know believes that it is a sad day when a visitor leaves his garden without something in a plastic bag.

Those new to an area, or new to gardening, are encouraged to get to know local gardeners, perhaps by joining a gardening club. This is the quickest way to learn about local idiosyncrasies of climate and soil, about prevailing local winds, or how quickly the local soil dries out, or which kinds of apple tree are most likely to survive the late frosts that are frequent.

The Internet works on a larger scale, but it too has facilities, called bulletin boards, where gardeners can exchange information, and is especially useful for those who are interested in particular groups of plants.

using information

Information is only useful once it is organized in an easily accessible format. Listing plants in table format is a useful way of making comparisons, perhaps with columns for flower color, soil conditions, etc.

A card index file is more flexible and allows you to sort through cards and lay them out on a flat surface to help develop planting schemes. A computer database provides the maximum power and flexibility, offering the opportunity to create fields for a whole range of plant characteristics and then to search rapidly for suggestions based on selection criteria such as "white, July-flowering, shade."

✳ **RELATED PAGES**

172 suggested reading
122 your plant notebook

example of plant notebook

plant name	type	flower color	foliage interest	approx. size	other information
Acer palmatum	Tree	n/a	Attractive foliage – red/purple in color	Approx. 3–12ft	Well-drained, but moist, soil
Berberis x lologensis	Shrub	Orange flowers in spring; blue-black berries in autumn	Glossy evergreen	Approx. 5ft	Ordinary garden soil
Achillea hybrids	Perennial	Wide range of bright colors	Aromatic	Approx. 1.5ft	Ordinary garden soil

plants and their needs

Plants need light, water and nutrients, but different plants are happy with different amounts or combinations.✻ Many plants have also adapted to difficult conditions. The obvious way to produce a successful garden in which plants thrive is to select plants that are naturally suited to your particular conditions.✻ Sometimes, however, this is neither possible nor desirable. Often we want to grow plants that need different conditions. It can be useful to think of plants as being either high-maintenance or low-maintenance.

high-input plants

When we want to get the most out of plants such as fruit and vegetables or cut flowers, we need to put in a lot to get results. The soil must be kept fertile and moist, and effort put into weeding, staking, watering, feeding and so on. Annuals and bedding plants that are replaced every year are labor-intensive, too, and make a heavy demand on the soil. This is what traditional gardening is all about – manipulating the environment to produce high yields.

low-input plants

These are plants that need relatively little maintenance, such as shrubs (if you do not keep them trimmed) and most perennials, although not highly bred ones like delphiniums and chrysanthemums. It makes sense for the majority of the area of a large garden to be planted with low-input plants, which have been chosen with the knowledge that they will thrive in the conditions in your garden. This will minimize the amount of soil preparation needed.

researching suitable plants

Visiting gardens and talking to other gardeners is a useful part of finding out about plants.✻ Another way of doing this is to consult reference books. The sheer amount of information in many gardening books can be quite intimidating. Some books include lists of plants for particular purposes, which can be helpful if you want to find plants for particular situations of light and soil type, that flower in particular seasons, or that have colored foliage or scented flowers. These lists are often found in the back of the book, and when used in conjunction with the main text are perhaps the most useful tool of all in drawing up lists.

size

The space needed for a plant to grow to its mature size is an important consideration in choosing plants for your garden, whether you will be planting directly into the ground or in containers. It is essential to do some research when thinking about planting trees and shrubs since you need to know how much space to allow for a particular variety.

below **Aconites** *(Eranthus hyemalis)* **and snowdrops** *(Galanthus nivalis)* **flourish beneath deciduous trees because they grow while the trees are leafless. Gardeners can utilize many adaptions that plants have made to their environment.**

You may decide that you are happy to plant an ultimately large tree in the garden, as long as it is fairly slow-growing. Perennials reach their mature size rapidly and can almost always be divided if they get too big; this is not possible with woody plants, which can only be kept small by annual trimming or pruning, which may be undesirable.

conditions

Plants are remarkably adaptable, and what is suggested in a book as the best conditions for a plant may often be broadly interpreted. Plants that are said to require moist conditions nearly always do well enough in ordinary garden soils, as long as they never dry out in hot summers; whereas those said to need dry conditions nearly always do better in an averagely moist soil, as long as it never gets waterlogged, especially in winter. In cooler climates, tender species that you are advised to bring inside in the winter often thrive outside in warm, sheltered places out of the worst of winter's frost and wind. Slightly less than hardy plants also require perfect drainage. Sun-loving plants usually grow well in a little shade, and shade-lovers generally do well in the sun. Compact, delicate or low, obviously slow-growing shade plants are genuinely more likely to need the shade, however. As a general rule, the more extreme your conditions, the more rigorous you should be in selecting those species that are suggested for those conditions.

using intuition

A little experience of plant-buying, aided by reference books or television programs, soon leads to a more intuitive sense of what will grow in your garden. Once you have gained this, you are well on the way to being truly "green-thumbed." Those who live in exposed conditions soon get the feel of those wiry, low-growing shrubs or grasses or perennials that can take whatever the weather throws at them, whereas the gardener with a rich soil soon learns to pick out lush plants, having learned the hard way that anything small and delicate will soon get swamped by the more competitive plants.

above **Some plants, such as these attractive yellow eremurus, will only thrive in perfect drainage. Most of the other plants are also adapted to flourish in drought-prone habitats.**

RELATED PAGES

14 site conditions

162 plant selector

13 discovering your taste

plant form and texture

above **The formality of clipped topiary shapes is complemented by exuberant plantings of annuals during the summer months.**

the informal borders they contain. Many gardeners want to include some of this kind of structure, such as low hedges of boxwood (Buxus) around borders, repeated planting of clipped boxwood in geometrical shapes, columns or pillars of yew, and bay trees trained as topiary or standards. A "standard" is a tree or shrub which by grafting or training is restricted to a single tree-like stem, usually shorter than normal and in which all growth is concentrated in a terminal crown of foliage. With the exception of standard trees or topiary, which may be easily purchased (albeit expensively), the clipped shapes are easy to make, if you are not too ambitious, and they only need trimming once a year.

Structure is the key to the long-term success of a garden. Flower color is so fleeting that, unless you are assured of a long season, often practicable only on a large scale, structural planting is the mainstay of continuity in the garden. Repetition is one of the keys to effective use of structural plants; think of columnar plants as being pillars in a building and you will have some idea of how the effective use of structural plants relies partly on their ability to create a sense of rhythm in a garden, and hence a sense of unity.

formality

The traditional formal garden has little other than structure, but looks as good in winter as it does in summer. The popularity of the twentieth-century English school of gardening is due in large part to its retention of many of the elements of classical formality – clipped hedges* and topiary – which form a permanent framework for the exuberance of

informality

Those less traditionally inclined may prefer to avoid such geometries, or perhaps to use them in a more adventurous and contemporary way. In the more informal garden, try using plants whose natural shapes are clear and defined. The Italian cypress (Cupressus sempervirens) is a fine example of the kind of narrowly vertical plant that can transform a garden by adding another dimension. Bamboos are useful structural plants, too; they are evergreen, and their canes add elegance to their surroundings. Many grasses are useful, if more seasonal, structural plants – many provide an important vertical dimension and some have soft, plumelike seedheads.

trees and shrubs

Small trees are often very useful for giving

structure to a garden, especially those with vertical branches or other distinct shapes such as a weeping habit. Those with interesting bark, such as many birches *(Betula)* and some cherries *(Prunus)* and maples *(Acer)*, are especially worth growing. On a smaller scale, many dwarf evergreen shrubs are useful structural plants, such as the very rounded types of hebe. The rounded habit of others, like lavenders *(Lavandula)*, may be accentuated by a minimum of annual clipping. Dwarf conifers, although overused, can be invaluable.

combining form and texture

Creating plant combinations involves both aesthetic and practical considerations. This is particularly the case with shapes. A grouping composed entirely of upwardly thrusting conifers would strike most observers as odd, and it would also be susceptible to weed invasion, as there would be no ground-layer plants. One made up entirely of spreading shapes would not have this problem, but would look rather boring, and there would be much more of a limit to the number of species that could be planted. Successful planting involves bringing together a variety of plant shapes that look attractive. Since plants rarely look good from top to bottom, this combining of different shapes enables you to hide the deficiencies of some with the good points of others; the bare lower stems of late-summer asters may be concealed with the rounded clumps of hardy geraniums, for example.

seasonal interest

The bringing together of different forms and textures is a vital way of making a planting interesting over a long season, one not just limited by flowering times. Forms are often more visible in winter, whereas textures are perhaps most noticeable just before plants flower. Some plants have soft, matt textures, such as the plumelike seedheads of many grasses; others are hard and dramatic, such as those with large or glossy leaves, spiky shapes or clearly defined flowerhead shapes. Contrasting textures is a more subtle way of designing combinations than working with form or color, yet it is vital for developing interesting and attractive plantings over the course of the year.

RELATED PAGES

38 hedges

below **Grasses are among the most dramatic of plants to consider when choosing plants to give structure over a long season: even in winter, with little other plant interest in the garden, they provide majestic focal points in the border.**

plant color

Another pair of contrasting attitudes towards color lies in the distinction between pastel shades and hot colors. Pastels – blues, mauves, pinks, creams and white, along with grey and silver foliage – make for a soothing atmosphere. They are rewarding in climates with frequent grey skies and subtle light, and there is a large number of plants to choose from, at least for early summer. Hot colors – yellows, oranges and reds – look best in stronger light, and there tend to be more plants with these colors towards the end of the summer.

color themes

Using color schemes is a very rewarding way to plant, and it is perhaps easiest for beginners to concentrate on color before considering form or texture. Single color scheme plantings can be particularly fun, as finding matching plants can be made into an enjoyable quest, but the overall effect may become rather dull. Plantings that are restricted to two or three colors are the next step, and are generally seen as livelier and more sophisticated. Schemes that involve more than two or three colors need more careful planning and often work best if a color theme is chosen for a particular season, and all other colors made to relate to it. This color theme could be expressed by one large dominating plant, or several of the same plant scattered throughout the planting, or by several different species with a similar color.

above **Blue and orange make a startling combination in the garden. How many strong mixtures are planted in the garden is a personal decision – some people love them, others find them tiring.**

Color is what gets most people excited in gardening. It also provokes a lot of lively disagreement, as views on color vary widely.✳ There are those who like harmony – matching colors, perhaps a limited color range, with nothing remotely jarring or clashing – and there are those who think contrast to be the spice of life, who enjoy mixing distinct colors and perhaps like to surprise with shocking combinations.

the color wheel

A good way to start analyzing your reactions to color, and to organize the way you plan with it, is to use the color wheel. The inner wheel represents the three primary colors and in between them the nine additional colors that you get by mixing them. Harmonies can be created by putting colors together that are next to each other, with more complex harmonies created by using other adjacent colors – up to five can be used before most eyes begin to see conflicts. Contrasts are created by putting together what are known as complementary colors: those opposite each other on the wheel. Pairs such as green and scarlet, blue and orange, yellow and purple, are vibrant, but in many cases work; that is, they contrast without looking as if they are competing for attention. The outer circle is made by mixing the colors of the inner circle with white; these are the pastel colors, which on the whole can be mixed with each other without clashes occurring.

Certain colors act as buffers, which means that they separate other, stronger colors, allowing them to be mixed successfully. Green, yellow-green, white and cream are buffers and explain why wildflower meadows successfully bring together lots of colors, including yellow and bright pink, which might otherwise clash. Not only are meadow flowers small and surrounded by lots of green, but there are a lot of less conspicuous cream and white flowers separating the bright ones. White flowers, especially when small but widely scattered, can perform a similar function in a border. White also brings light into a planting scheme, which may be useful if reds and purples have made it dark. This is part of the role of white in traditional red, white and blue summer bedding schemes. Gray or silver foliage can be used as well and looks good with all colors except yellow, which can look muddy if placed next to gray.

left Colored foliage has the advantage of a long season. The yellow grass hakenochloa mixes with autumn colors, and a sharply contrasting pink phormium variety.

below While some people have the ability to combine colors instinctively, others may find it useful to refer to a color wheel.

RELATED PAGES

13 discovering your taste

combining plants

Borders and other plantings that involve combining a number of different plants can be challenging, but they are always satisfying to create. The essence of the exercise is to match up the plants that you have shortlisted;* this may result in some being rejected, but you may also discover a need for others you had not thought of. When combining plants, you need to consider a number of criteria: form (the shape of the plant), texture (of foliage or flower), color, leaf shape, season of flowering and position (this includes cultural considerations, such as whether your chosen plants will be happy growing next to each other).

planting styles

Tastes in gardening vary as much as they do in any other sphere. What is important is that you do what you feel is right, plant what you want to plant. Far too many people plan their gardens on the basis of what they think is fashionable, or what they think they ought to do. We have already seen how gardens can be placed on a spectrum between the strictly formal and the wildly informal.* Another way of broadly categorizing planting styles is between harmony and contrast. Harmonious planting aims at emphasizing similarities, such as planting a border with only one color, and complementary qualities. Contrasting

right **The shape and texture of the small fluffy heads of the grass *Lagurus ovatus* echo the summer foliage of *Bassia scoparia* behind, yet their sizes are dramatically different.**

planting stimulates the eye by juxtaposing quite different colors or shapes, creating a sense of drama and excitement.

learning to combine plants

Most people notice color first, so it can take some practice to look at combining plant forms and textures. With pencil and paper, draw rough outlines of the shapes of plants you are planning to work with. It is harder to be diagrammatic with textures, but you could try various kinds of shading.

❶

visualizing combinations

Too many soft textures or plants without any outstanding shape or form can make a planting quite dull. Taking black-and-white photographs of established borders is one way of analyzing this; without the distraction of color, it is possible to see how effectively form and texture work together.

Combinations of dramatic, striking foliage with quiet, soft leaf shapes and textures – for example, contrasting vertical, linear leaves (such as iris) or large, glossy ones (such as bergenias) with more common small-leaved plants – are usually successful.

defining plant categories

It is a good idea to list your desired plants, and then define your own categories of shape and texture. You might end up with something like this:

▸ Plant shapes – vertical, pyramidal, round, horizontal, vaselike, pendent, conical, sprawling;

▸ Leaf shapes and textures – soft, spiky, linear, rounded, thistlelike, glossy, matt, coarse;

▸ Flower shapes – daisies, buttons, spikes, spires, catkins, clouds, balls, bells, trumpets.

You can then refer to these categories when planning your plantings. When matching colors, for example, use them to ensure that there is variety in shape or texture; or, perhaps, if color of flowers or foliage does not interest you so much, use these categories as the primary focus of your plant combinations.

❷

left and below **Simple line drawings can help to organize thoughts about plant shapes. ❶ represents a mixture that may be too dynamic and restless for some, whereas ❷ involves more rounded and restful shapes.**

❋   **RELATED PAGES**

108 using a plant notebook

10 garden styles

planning planting schemes

Planning a planting involves juggling lots of different elements: color schemes, form and texture, cultural conditions, the seasons. The easiest way to start is to make a list of favored plants and then taking the aspect that interests you most, color perhaps, draw up a plan,* and then think about what you have decided in the light of the other factors. There are a number of other aspects of planting that should be considered including height and plant numbers. How one uses these often depends on the function of the area to be planted.

types of planting

Borders are literally that, an edge, with a backdrop of some kind, such as a fence or wall. Traditionally plants in borders have been planted in descending order of height, with the tallest at the back and shortest at the front, although in practice this rule is frequently relaxed, as long as plants that flower are not hidden by taller neighbors.

Island beds are freestanding borders usually planted around taller, often shrubby specimens in the center, with lawn or paving all around them.

Open borders are island beds on a larger scale, or even whole gardens where there is no lawn, only plants, generally perennials rather than shrubs, filling the whole area. Cottage gardens often adopt this style.*

height

It is easiest to plant so that taller plants are at the rear or center of a planting and shorter ones at the front; this at least allows everything to be seen. However, since early perennials and bulbs are short and late-flowering perennials generally tall, this can be rather limiting. Putting some bulbs and shade-tolerant early perennials towards the back will help to spread spring interest more evenly. This is particularly useful for hiding plants that look scruffy after flowering. Scattering some taller plants throughout a planting, especially if they are quite narrow and upright, creates a more relaxed and natural feeling than having a strict graduation of heights.

right **A narrow border may seem limiting to plant. However, extending it into the sky, with obelisks supporting young climbers, and bushy evergreens like** *Euphorbia characias*, **will make the most of it.**

RELATED PAGES

30 your garden plan

10 garden styles

left **Wide borders offer great opportunities for combining big clumps of perennials and ornamental grasses, especially the expansive later-flowering varieties.**

below **An early-summer planting of pastel shades is especially popular. A great variety of plants can be used and good results are easy to achieve.**

grouping plants

Some types of plants are so big and/or imposing that there may only be room for one of them in a border, an example being a solitary pampas grass *(Cortaderia selloana)* in an island bed. Others have to be grouped to create any impact at all. These include small ground cover plants and spire-shaped flower spikes such as foxgloves *(Digitalis)*, which look lonely on their own. They do not need to be in a tight clump, just grouped closely enough to be seen to relate to each other. Some plants look much better if they are surrounded by other much smaller varieties, very upright grasses for example or anything with a distinct and noble habit.

It is common practice to group plants in clumps when planting several of the same variety, using odd rather than even numbers. A more natural and carefree effect is achieved by blending and intermingling different varieties, more appropriate perhaps if species plants are being used rather than hybrids. Scattering a number of the same variety across a planting can also create a greater overall impact than putting them all in one clump. Repeating favorite color combinations throughout a planting scheme can be particularly striking.

planting calendars

A calendar✱ is a useful tool for selecting plants. It enables you to see at a glance what will be in flower at any one time, what color combinations there will be at that time, and what gaps there may be through the year.

List favorite plants down the side of the chart and times of the year across the top. Draw a line to indicate the flowering period of each plant, colored to approximate flower color; a dotted line can indicate reduced flowering or uncertainty. This applies to plants where, for example, in a mild autumn, flowering may continue when it would normally be over. Lines can also be used to represent attractive foliage or other qualities

such as berries. Some gardening books are rather vague about flowering times, which is where a notebook✱ and your own research can yield more precise figures. Nursery catalogs with good descriptive sections are often more precise than books. If you have noted particularly effective planting schemes in your notebook, or have accumulated lists of a number of favorite combinations that you have seen on particular dates, then it is possible to mark these dates on the calendar and use them as a basis for planning the rest of the border.

Using plants or combinations that you know well, like and feel confident about is a good basis for planning. They can be used as theme plants, to set the tone for a particular time of year, with others chosen to fit in and complement them. A theme plant should be a strong color, otherwise it may get overshadowed by others, unless you are able to use a lot of it, as with pale-flowered bulbs for example, which could be widely scattered. Theme plants for different seasons are indicated here.

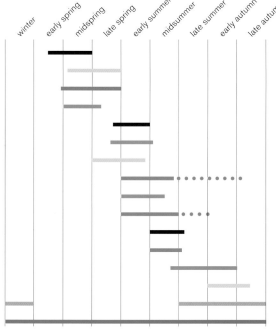

notebook
creative planting

This chapter has explained how to combine plants to make the most of their form, texture, color and scent. The following pages provide space in which to record your own favorite plants and plan successful combinations.

your plant notebook

Use this table to record the plants you have seen and liked. You may want to write down more names than there is space for here, in which case you can photocopy this and the following page.

plant name	type	flower color	foliage interest	approx. size	other information

plant name	type	flower color	foliage interest	approx. size	other information

your plant color calendar

Use this chart to plan plant color combinations with colored pencils, following the example of the chart on page 120.

plant name	winter	early spring	midspring	late spring	early summer	midsummer	late summer	early autumn	late autumn

plant name	winter	early spring	midspring	late spring	early summer	midsummer	late summer	early autumn	late autumn

plan your planting scheme

Use this space to plan a planting scheme, following the advice throughout this chapter on combining plants to best effect.

site survey

site measurements:

soil conditions:

aspect/temperature:

existing planting:

action plan

plants required:

address book:

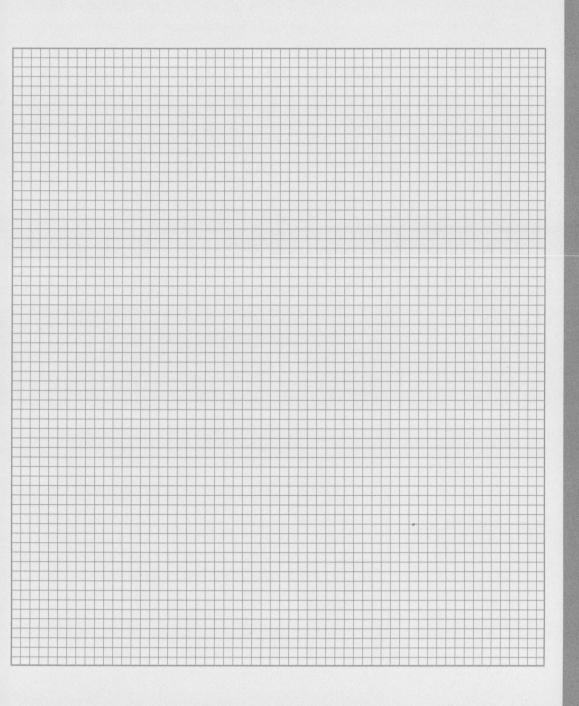

planting
practicalities

Traditional gardening advice leans heavily towards soil improvement, and even today it may be useful – the secret is to know when radical measures are necessary. Why put in all that work when your garden may grow better without?

soil preparation and planting

prepare the ground thoroughly for trees, shrubs and climbers than it is for border perennials or temporary plants such as annuals.

removing weeds

The elimination of perennial weeds (those which live from year to year) is fundamental to the success of any kind of planting. Digging the ground over, and picking weed roots out by hand, is often ineffective, quite apart from being incredibly slow. Many perennial weeds will regenerate from the tiniest scrap of root. Weedkillers may seem an obvious solution, but many fear their long-term effects. Those based on glyphosate and ammonium sulphamate are safe and effective, however, and they break down rapidly in the soil. Some weeds – stinging nettles for example – may remain after application of the safer weedkillers and may have to be dealt with by other methods.

One of the most effective ways of killing all perennial weeds is to smother them with sheets of black plastic, which are laid on the ground in spring with their edges buried. By

above **Lupins** *(Lupinus)* **and candelabra primulas form a colorful planting. Lush-growing varieties like this need relatively high soil moisture and fertile conditions; they would benefit from the addition of plenty of compost.**

Once you have matched the right plant to the right site and conditions, it is essential to prepare the soil before planting. The extent to which you do this, however, depends on the type of plant you are planning to grow. Because woody plants make a big investment simply in producing wood and tend to adapt more slowly to shocks, such as being transplanted, it is far more important to

late autumn, practically all the weeds underneath will be dead. Some gardeners use old carpet or even newspapers instead.

hoeing and mulching

Land that is cleared of perennial weeds may still sprout remarkable crops of weeds from seed, although most of these will be annuals. Hoeing every few weeks will kill the seedlings, and if this is carried out over the space of a summer, the "seed bank" in the top layer of soil will be greatly depleted, unless more are floating in on the breeze from neighboring gardens or wild areas. Mulching after planting, using bark chips or similar products, is perhaps the best means of preventing weed seed germination around new plants.✳

soil improvement

Many gardeners labor long and hard to prepare large areas of ground for new borders or other areas of planting. This is often not necessary and may sometimes be counterproductive.✳ However, the site for a vegetable garden, or for a permanent planting of soft fruit like strawberries or raspberries, certainly benefits from a thorough working-over of the ground. It is somewhat true where fruit and vegetables are concerned that the more you put in the more you get out. Removal of weed roots must be total, and if the soil is less than perfect, the more composted manure or other organic matter you add the better. If the ground is to be used for growing bedding

above **Gardens can be created in the most unpromising of places, as long as the plants are chosen with some degree of knowledge of their requirements.**

left **Woody plants like this standard gooseberry benefit from thorough soil preparation, as they are slower to establish than herbaceous plants.**

 RELATED PAGES

152 mulches

16 analyzing the site

plants and annuals, there is a point to soil improvement too, as these are fast-growing plants that need rich soil to perform well over the whole growing season.

The larger-growing, later-flowering perennials, and traditional favorites like delphiniums and chrysanthemums, do benefit from well-prepared and well-fed soil. However, unless the soil is particularly poor it is not worth carrying out large-scale soil improvement for the majority of perennials. Breaking up the soil by digging and rototilling

may only bring previously dormant weed seed to the surface, while widespread use of fertilizers will help the resulting weeds to grow even better. Smaller perennials, many shrubs, conifers and heathers will grow more quickly in well-prepared soils, but do not benefit dramatically, because they often originate from very impoverished environments. Good planting procedures and aftercare are more important to shrubs than heavy soil improvement.

below **Hardy perennials catmint** *(Nepeta x faassenii)* **and** *Geranium sanguineum* **can be mixed with annuals such as California poppy** *(Eschscholzia)* **for a rapid and colorful effect.**

improving soil structure, which can be permanent once achieved. There are various compounds, often based on gypsum or seaweed, that will help to open up clay soils, but price usually limits their use to small areas.✳

planting shrubs

To prepare the ground for planting woody plants, break up the soil around and below where the plant's present root system is to go. This will make it easy for young roots to penetrate into the soil and help the plant to establish. Adding fertilizer at this stage does not help, unless the soil is very poor, since it is better for roots to venture out and find their own nutrients. Adding compost or peat moss can be counterproductive, too, creating soggy root conditions that are conducive to fungal attack on damaged roots.

All plants grown in lightweight composts, which includes the majority of those bought in garden centers, should have some of their roots loosened from the root ball before planting. Spreading roots out in the planting hole also helps, especially on the heavy soils which are such a contrast to the potting compost in which the plant was raised.

left **This gravel garden✳ is a perfect example of how colorful plantings can be achieved by mixing groups of perennials which all have similar requirements.**

improving soil types

Sandy and very light soils tend to be poor and to dry out quickly. If you want to grow plants that need a better soil type, organic matter in large quantities will be needed; use well-rotted manure or any kind of decayed vegetable matter. Since these soils seem to have a never-ending hunger for such material, work on soil improvement only in key areas.

Clay soils are the probably the old-fashioned gardener's least favorite kind. They may be hard to work – sticky as glue in winter, hard as concrete in summer – but roses thrive on them, as do many perennials. The secret is to avoid digging them up after planting, limiting attempts at soil improvement to key areas such as vegetable plots. Organic matter is again the key to

✳ **RELATED PAGES**

14 site conditions
58 gravel garden

project: planting a tree

Bare-rooted trees and shrubs must be planted when dormant (without leaves in the winter), but those grown in containers may be transplanted at any time except during drought or frost, as long as they are watered periodically after planting.

tools • spade • watering can • fork • hammer

materials • suitable tree • tree tie • 4ft stake • organic matter or compost

1 Make sure that your selected site will provide your young tree with enough light and shelter, but conversely that your adult tree will not be cramped, at either root or branch level. Remove all plant growth from the area to eliminate any potential competition for nutrients. Water your tree in its container so that the compost is thoroughly moist. Dig a hole about twice the width of the root ball and as deep as is practicable (at least one and a half times the depth of the contained roots), but not so deep that you will deprive the roots of oxygen. Break up the soil at the base of the hole with a fork, particularly in areas with heavy, sticky soil.

4

planting for the future

Careful planning will ensure that you choose a tree that satisfies your functional and aesthetic needs. Trees can be used to screen buildings and roads; they can provide shelter and deaden intrusive noise, but do not select too big or too thorny a tree if your garden is small, and try to find a variety with two seasons of interest. Probably the most expensive option, container-grown trees are ideal if you want to create instant height and structure, or an established feel, in a new garden; they tend to get established more quickly than bare-rooted specimens because their roots are less disturbed.

2 Hammer in the stake just off center toward the direction of the wind before you plant your tree, to avoid damaging the root ball. Lie the pot on its side and slide out the tree. Gently loosen the roots and remove weeds. Hold the young tree in position in the hole, with the roots spread out, and check on the planting depth. Then backfill the hole with the displaced topsoil and some organic matter, the new soil level coming as close as possible to the original one (usually visible on the trunk).

3 Use your heel to firm the soil around the trunk, ensuring good contact between roots and soil and reducing the risk of wind damage. If you tread too heavily, however, you will compact the soil and impede drainage.

4 Attach the trunk to the stake with a tree tie – firmly enough to support it against wind while the roots take hold, but allowing for some movement. After a year you will probably need to loosen the tie. Increase the number of ties for tall trees, or if your site is very windy.

herbaceous and bedding plants

These are the plants that provide most of the color in the garden, especially in the latter half of the growing season. The development and marketing of new cultivars is continual, making this a dynamic and exciting area in gardening.

perennials

"Herbaceous" or "hardy" perennials, usually known simply as perennials,* go through an annual cycle of growth, often producing a lot of both top and root growth, which dies down every autumn, to be replaced the following spring. While some stay the same spread all their lives, most long-lived perennials gradually increase in size, spreading outwards to form large clumps.

below **Foxgloves (Digitalis purpurea) are biennial: they live for two years only. They set a great deal of seed however, so the species usually stays in the garden. Delphiniums (right) are perennial, so they come back every year.**

Herbaceous plants establish far more quickly than woody plants, and little soil preparation is needed on good soils. Heavy soils should be broken up around the young plants, and on poor ones, some nutrients, especially those that are rich in phosphorus, which moves very slowly through the soil, can be dug in just below the new plant to help it through its first few years.

Once established, most perennials are easy to maintain, although they involve more work than shrubs. This is because of all the dead growth that is produced in the autumn, which needs tidying up. Traditionally, this was done quickly, leaving bare borders all winter long. Modern practice favors a minimum trimming, leaving the dead seedheads on the stems until late winter. Many perennials and ornamental grasses have very decorative seedheads, and the seed is much appreciated by birds. It is important that all this top growth is returned to the border at some stage, otherwise nutrients will be gradually lost. It can be composted or put through a shredder, and then returned as a mulch around the plants.

In garden centers, perennials are sold either as plants in pots or as dormant roots in plastic bags in winter and spring. Perennials can also be grown from seed, although it can be a slow process. The later-flowering, taller types never look good in containers, and so are rarely sold this way. Since they die back in winter, they are an ideal product for mail order, and this is the best means of buying perennials; nurseries that sell them in this way usually stock a wider range than garden centers.

Perennials may be transplanted more or less at any time while they are dormant. In regions with a mild winter climate, autumn transplanting is best as the plants have an opportunity to settle in and make some root growth over the winter. Transplanting should be left until spring in climates with regular severe winters.

Given their rate of spread, it is easy to propagate perennials by division, and many gardens have been stocked entirely by donations from the borders of friends and relatives, perhaps complemented with a few purchased plants. Ease of propagation also means that established plants can be multiplied and moved around the garden.

above With careful planning, late summer can be a very colorful time in the garden, with the widest variety of perennials in flower. Here dramatic yellow helenium grows alongside drifts of scarlet crocosmia and distinctive stands of purple-and-white acanthus.

left Many perennials, such as these white argyranthemums, spread rapidly and will eventually make fairly large bushes. For the more impatient, they are easily propagated by cuttings in early spring or late summer.✳

✳ **RELATED PAGES**

106 plant types
142 propagating plants
144 taking cuttings

hardy annuals

These are the traditional cottage garden flowers such as English marigolds (*Calendula*), love-in-a-mist *(Nigella)* and larkspur *(Consolida)*, along with an increasing range of new cultivars.✳ They can be sown outside, straight into the positions where they are to flower. So long as the seedlings are protected from slugs and snails and kept watered they are remarkably easy and rewarding. You should also avoid pulling them up by mistake for weeds when they are small. Thinning out, to avoid the overcrowding which can restrict healthy plant growth, will help to produce plants that grow lushly and flower over a much longer period.

half-hardy annuals
(bedding plants)

So-called "half-hardy annuals" are raised under cover and sold as young plants in late spring and early summer for "bedding out" in the summer. They are traditionally planted in geometric patterns with brightly contrasting colors. Buying plants in this way certainly reduces the element of risk, as well as the need for forward planning that is inherent in growing from seed in the open ground. The range of plants is more restricted, though, and they are regarded by many as garish and overblown – for example, French marigolds *(Tagetes)*, begonias and petunias. These plants are frequently featured in hanging baskets and containers, too, and are useful for adding a seasonal splash of color to dull areas.

patio plants

Sold alongside the bedding plants are those like pelargoniums (usually incorrectly called geraniums) which are in fact perennials, but are not winter hardy. Their numbers have grown considerably in recent years through the development of a whole range often called "patio plants," nearly all of which are frost-tender perennials such as marguerites *(Argyranthemum)*, diascias and penstemons. These are mostly fast-growing and long-flowering, making them an exciting alternative to the traditional bedding plants, and one with quite a different appearance, more natural and free-flowing, with a much wider color range. Many also make good hanging-basket and container plants. Their numbers are joined by some excellent summer foliage plants such as the silver *Lotus bertholettii.*

Since most of these patio plants are potentially perennial, many gardeners try to keep them from year to year. This is a wise course of action if you are not sure whether you would be able to buy them again. Plants can be dug up in autumn, cut hard back and grown in pots in cold rooms inside, in greenhouses or in a well-ventilated cold frame, over the winter. Most will survive light frosts, if kept on the dry side. Alternatively, cuttings may be taken in summer and overwintered, indoors on a windowsill if necessary, and planted the following spring. Most are very easily propagated from cuttings.

 RELATED PAGES

106 plant types

144 taking cuttings

far left above **English marigolds** *(Calendula officinalis)* **are one of the easiest of all annuals to grow, often self-sowing year after year.**

far left below **Love-in-a-mist** *(Nigella damascena)* **is another very easy annual, which is sown where it is to flower, to bloom several months later.**

left **Half-hardy plants like these flower for most of the summer, but will need to be brought indoors before the first hard frosts.**

project: planting scheme

A good way to establish the number and type of plants you need is to sketch a planting scheme on paper. You can then "redraw" your design on the ground by means of a string grid, twine lines on the site corresponding to lines on the plan.

tools • garden twine and stakes • measuring tape • spade or fork • plant tags

materials • perennials such as asters, poppies, bellflowers and yarrow

1 Employing the scale that you used to draw your planting plan, stretch a series of taut lines of twine across the ground between stakes positioned at the edges, forming a grid that corresponds to the grid on your paperwork. You can leave this grid in place for as long as you like, thereby extending the period of time you have at your disposal for planting – several months, if necessary. Each of the squares of our grid measures 1 x 1yd. Use plant tags to mark any existing plants which cannot be seen: dormant perennials or bulbs, for example. In this way you will be able to avoid disturbing them when you start to plant your new plants.

planning and planting

On your planting plan remember to take into account the finished height, shape and color of each component plant, for this is all you will have for reference if you, as we did, plant your plot during the winter months, when many dormant perennials can be obtained from nurseries or by mail order – supplied as bare roots in a small bag of earth. Be careful not to lose the labels because even if you do recognize the roots of a particular plant, you have no way of knowing its color. Remember too that the apparently large areas of bare earth will soon be filled by abundant growth: give your plants plenty of space to grow rather than overcrowding them.

2 Lay out your plants ready for planting, their locations within each square reflecting their position in the squares of the paper plan. If it is windy or dry, woody plants and perennials should be planted as soon as possible. Wet or humid winter weather, however, gives you time to rethink and adjust your plan as you work, since perennials can be left out in these conditions for several days without being harmed.

3 Break up the ground below and around each plant's new home with a spade or fork to enable the roots to make good contact with the soil and to penetrate it easily.

4 Spread out the roots of each plant in its planting hole, then backfill the hole with broken soil and use your heel to firm it. Woody plants should be transplanted so that the new soil level corresponds closely to its original level – usually a mark visible on the main stem – while perennials should be planted more deeply than they were before. Tag each plant as you proceed, to avoid accidentally digging them up later or standing on newly planted roots.

propagating plants

The easiest and most popular methods of propagation for the amateur gardener are division, taking cuttings, and growing plants from seed. New plants, when rooted, can be grown either in pots or in a special nursery bed until ready for planting out.

above **Hardy species of geranium or cranesbill are very easy to grow, especially the pink G. cinereum types that can be dug up and divided after being in the ground only a year or two.**

division

This is suitable for clump-forming perennials and produces instant new plants. Divide the clump by lifting and carefully pulling it apart to produce several pieces, each with a shoot or obvious bud and some roots. The divisions can then be planted directly into the garden or grown in a nursery bed. Older, tougher plants may need splitting by means of two garden forks inserted back-to-back into the clump. Division can be done at any time over the winter or in early spring, but should be left to spring for anything that seems less robust, and for most ornamental grasses.

taking cuttings

Many shrubs and perennials can be propagated by cuttings.✱ Some plants root very easily, others only with great difficulty. The two most common types of cutting are:
▸ Stem cuttings – the conventional type of cutting. The top of a stem of the current year's growth, with several leaves on it, is cut off through a node, the point where leaves join the stem. The best time to take stem cuttings is at the "semiripe" stage, that is when the young shoots are still growing but are beginning to harden. If the stem is long enough, a whole series of cuttings may be made from its length, as well as from the tip. Anything with two nodes (one cut through and one with some leaves) may "take," the dormant buds at the base of the upper leaf stems growing into new shoots.
▸ Heel cuttings involve removing a young stem together with a sliver, or heel, of the parent stem. This technique is particularly useful for propagating perennials when they start growing in spring, as the young shoots are full of growth hormones and root quickly.

rooting cuttings

Prepare the cutting by trimming off any leaves that might otherwise be below compost level. There are various hormone-based rooting compounds available, which are worth applying to the base of the cutting if the instructions are followed carefully. Insert the cutting in a pot of sterilized compost that is very open and free-draining, made by mixing potting compost with a quarter to a half by volume of sand, vermiculite or, best of all, perlite. Place the pot in a position where the cuttings will receive good, indirect light. They are at great risk of drying out, so they should either be placed in a cold frame and kept moist, or in clear plastic bags to keep a high degree of humidity around them. If plastic bags are used, ventilation will be reduced with a consequent danger of fungal rot setting in; to prevent this, open the bags every few days and remove any dead leaves. Rooting cuttings may take from ten days to many months depending on the plant. Once rooted, the young plants should be potted and kept well watered until established.

seeds

Growing plants from seed is one of the most satisfying parts of gardening. Nearly all vegetables are grown from seed, as are many annuals; most perennials can be, although amateur gardeners usually do not bother. If you want lots of perennials and have a tight budget, though, seed is a very good way of getting them. The germination of most woody plants and some perennials is slow and problematic, but is covered by a number of specialist books.

germinating seeds

Sowing instructions are usually given on seed packets. Some plants from warm climates, such as tomatoes and petunias, need to be started off in warm conditions indoors between late winter and the middle of spring; others can be sown in pots or in a seedbed outside. Seeds need moisture and the right temperature in order to germinate, and seedlings need light. If you sow seeds inside the house, rather than in a greenhouse, it will be a problem giving them enough light, while a sunny windowsill may

dry them out very fast. Try to find a window where they will grow without getting too leggy, but which is out of direct sun for most of the day.

In the case of seed where there is little in the packet and which is therefore precious, sowing in containers of potting compost will ensure that you can keep an eye on them and make sure that they are watered regularly. Putting the pots into plastic bags will keep them moist, although they must be checked regularly and the bag removed as soon as germination starts. Seed trays and young seedlings must be kept in light shade.

using a seedbed

Some vegetables, such as cabbage and broccoli, and perennials are often sown in a seedbed in which the soil is well broken up and which can be watered if necessary, since small seedlings are very prone to drying out, and then transplanted. This should be done sooner rather than later, since young plants adapt more quickly, and after being well watered and in the evening. Watering and protection from slugs are needed for the first weeks after transplanting.

nursery beds

A nursery bed is a part of the garden with well-cultivated soil where young plants can be grown for their first few months or year. The soil needs to be absolutely weed-free, well broken up (not lumpy), in light shade and near a source of water.

above **Many gardeners save their own seed from year to year, which is very satisfying and saves money. Opium poppies (Papaver somniferum) have large capsules from which seed can be shaken easily.**

 RELATED PAGES

144 taking cuttings

project: taking cuttings

Once you understand the principles, taking cuttings is a relatively easy way to propagate many shrubs and perennials. It is also inexpensive, giving you the means to acquire plants you might not be able to afford as full-grown specimens.

tools • pruners

materials • sterile compost • perlite • hormone rooting powder • clean pots

1 Assemble your tools and materials. Then create well-aerated rooting conditions for your cuttings, by mixing one part perlite to three parts compost by volume. Fill your flower pots.

2 Take your cutting material from a healthy mother plant. Select nonflowering shoots: root-producing hormones are suppressed by flower-producing ones, so shoots with flower buds are less likely to root as well or as quickly.

3 Trim the cuttings: cut the stem at the node – where the leaf joins the stem – where the growth hormones are concentrated in the node. To have a good, clean stem to insert into

4

when to try

Stem cuttings – as opposed to leaf or root cuttings – are best taken in late summer when the stems are "semiripe," older and less likely to wilt. If you are trying to propagate cuttings from plants that are difficult to root, however, it is best to start early, because some can take months and it is best to give the cuttings time to mature before the arrival of winter's more difficult growing conditions. You must water these regularly, checking for disease and removing any dead or moldy leaves. Once they have rooted, pot your new plants individually and, if you have been growing them inside, move them outside gradually, or your efforts will be wasted.

the compost, now gently pull from the main stem all except three full-sized leaves (essential for photosynthesis) and any unavoidable flowers and buds. You can also "wound" some cuttings before planting them to stimulate growth, by removing a sliver of bark from the lowest inch to expose more of the node.

4 Dip the base of the cutting in rooting powder. Shake off and discard the excess before inserting the cuttings in the compost. Ensure that they are not touching each other to minimize the spread of infection, should one cutting succumb to mold, for example. Water the cuttings and put them in a light but cool spot, away from direct sunlight: a mist-unit propagator is ideal, but a cool, shaded cold frame or even a cool inside windowsill suffices. If your cuttings wilt, increase the humidity by putting a loose plastic bag over them, but remove it regularly to let the air circulate. The easiest cuttings will take about ten days to root: renewed shoot growth is a sure indication that your cuttings have rooted: pulling on them is not a good idea since it might damage any new roots.

containers

Containers allow those who have very little or no soil area to grow plants, but they also offer all gardeners a great deal of flexibility. Containers allow you to put plants exactly where you want them, however temporarily. Pots full of flowers can be placed in strategic positions around the garden if there is a lack of color at any time. Containers are also useful if you like to entertain, allowing you to move plants around to get the best possible effect for your guests.

Those with concrete rather than soil may want to grow plants permanently in containers. This can be done, but not all plants like it, and therefore you should research your plants thoroughly. Those with a shallow rooting system, like camellias, rhododendrons and heathers, are usually the most successful. Permanent container plants can act as the framework to your garden and be added to seasonally – polyanthus and bulbs in spring, annuals in summer, and winter-flowering pansies in winter.

Success with containers results from remembering to water regularly, and starting off the season by adding some long-lasting feed to the compost. This will supply plenty of nutrients and save you having to feed every week. Deadheading is also important; removing the dead flowers helps to keep more coming.

improvising

While there is a wealth of flowerpots and windowboxes, it is also possible to improvise and make your own, adapting such things as water tanks, industrial containers and barrels. Any reasonably strong container that can have the all-important drainage holes drilled in the bottom, and has not contained toxic chemicals, can be used to hold plants. Unsightly containers may be hidden by bricks, wrapped in burlap or surrounded by smaller pots. One of the most attractive uses

above Containers are marvelous for creating instant effects such as this, where blue hyacinths (Hyacinthus) and yellow daffodils (Narcissus) decorate a flight of steps.

right **All sorts of containers can be used for plants, although they should always have holes made in them to allow for water drainage.**

left **Containers allow the adventurous to experiment with all sorts of unconventional plant material, such as these ornamental grasses, which contrast effectively with the shapes of the pots.**

of old materials is the sink garden, where rock garden plants and dwarf bulbs are grown in old sinks. While old stone sinks now cost a fortune, it is possible to coat modern sinks with "hypertufa," a mixture of cement and potting compost, which makes them look more like the real thing. The great thing about sink gardens is the sheer number of plant species you can pack in, including many beautiful and exciting alpines.

planting for color

For many people, container gardening is all about a profusion of summer color: petunias tumbling out of hanging baskets, pelargoniums and lobelia gushing from large terracotta pots. Annuals and patio plants are the plants that really make summer on a terrace, with their rapid growth and long flowering season. Faced with a profusion of plants in garden centers and nurseries to choose from, it is easy to get carried away and cram too many differently colored plants in the same pot, yet the most effective containers are those that use only a limited number of plants within a strict color scheme. Try to use a few theme plants; for example, you could base your container display around plants with silver or purple leaves, which have an especially long season. Scatter them around your pots and you will effectively tie everything together visually.

✷   **RELATED PAGES**

114 plant color
139 patio plants

project: planting containers

Containers offer tremendous scope. You can work on many levels, with troughs, pots, hanging baskets and windowboxes; change your look whenever you like by rearranging your pots or replanting; and juxtapose plants that like different soils.

tools • potting compost • trowel • suitable container

materials • patio plants such as verbenas, brachycome, penstemon, geranium and diascia

1 Select your containers and assemble your tools and materials. Provided that your proposed container has drainage holes, almost anything can be used and can either play a major role in the display or may be made completely subordinate to the planting, disguised by trailing flowers and leaves. Use pot-grown plants if you want an immediate display; they are also good because they will not outgrow the container during the flowering season. Plan where you will position the plants carefully, bearing in mind their height, habit and color. Fill your container halfway with compost specifically prepared for containers; this will contain plenty of nutrients so that your plants

will not need feeding during their first season. If the plants are going to be tightly packed, a long-life fertilizer pellet may be a good idea. The traditional practice of putting pieces of broken flowerpot over the drainage hole is unnecessary.

2 Water your plants well before you plant them, then remove each from its pot, and loosen the roots before scooping back the compost and placing the plant in position. Pat the compost gently around each plant, being careful not to leave air pockets, but making sure that the compost is not compacted, as this will result in compaction and consequent poor root growth – shaking or banging the container is a better way to settle the compost around the roots. Add more moist compost, if necessary, ensuring that the necks of your plants are about ½in below the rim of your container, and that the top of the compost is level.

3 Once your containers are planted, water them thoroughly to moisten the compost and to help it settle. And remember that regular watering is essential throughout the season.

when to try

Most annuals can be grown in containers to provide a colorful, long-lasting summer display or to complement other plants, and a surprising number can be fitted into one pot. Be careful, however, to choose your plants with your proposed site in mind – how sunny, windy and shady it is. Many herbs flourish in containers so you need never be short of culinary flavors; you would even be able to move them inside during cold periods. If space is at a real premium, parsley, marjoram, thyme and chives would combine well in a windowbox, but if you have room for a selection of pots, rosemary and bay look good grown as single specimens.

gardening to eat

right **This chart is intended as a basic guide to organizing the growing of vegetables. More information can be found in specialist books, and instructions are usually printed on seed packets.**

The heading "plant" refers primarily to those vegetables that are usually grown from seed and then transplanted into their final positions.

The heading "problems" refers only to those problems that can more or less wipe out a crop, to which a particular vegetable is specifically prone. It does not mean that those without an entry are trouble-free.

Producing your own food can be immensely satisfying. Even a small plot can be productive enough to make an effect on the family budget, and you can also grow crops that are unavailable commercially. Equally important is the recognition that so much of what we eat has been chemically treated. Even if we are not strictly organic in our approach, we know where it has been.

small gardens

Some of the most popular plants to grow are salad crops like lettuce and tomatoes, where freshness and flavor are crucial, and even a windowsill has enough space for pots of herbs. The key to maximum productivity is good organization, which ensures that space is never wasted. Even the smallest garden can accommodate strawberries, a slightly larger one cane fruit such as raspberries or bush fruit such as gooseberries. Apples on dwarfing rootstocks can be grown in small gardens, while other tree fruit – cherries, pears and so on – needs more space.

conditions

Edible plants are often bred for very specific conditions, to crop well in a particular region for example, and may not produce so much in an area with a different soil type or climate. It is especially important that fruit trees are carefully chosen; go for types that you know do well in your area. Warm-season plants may have hybrids specially bred for growing outside.

cropping time

Fruit and vegetables are bred to be harvested at different times, so if you are buying more than one hybrid, choose ones that can be harvested at different times. Early vegetables are especially important, as produce in the first part of the season is always welcome.

new and old hybrids

Most fruit and vegetable plants are hybrids, but some vegetables are sold as "F1" hybrids, which means that the seed is produced in precise conditions and that the crop will be highly uniform. But the home gardener does not always want uniformity. "Heirloom" or older types of vegetables and fruit have been revived recently; many have distinctive flavors, while others look attractive or just different. They do not yield as much as modern hybrids, however, and are more likely to suffer from pests and diseases.

fruit trees

Many fruit trees are not self-pollinating and won't produce fruit unless pollinated by another tree of the same type; others have separate male and female plants. A self-pollinating variety does not need a pollinator, but may yield better if able to cross with another. Fruit trees are grafted: the root is from a different type of plant to the one above ground. Rootstocks vary in how large they allow the tree to grow, so choosing the right one is a fundamental decision. Read labels and catalogs carefully and always buy from a specialized nursery.

vegetable	sow	plant	harvest	problems
Fava beans	Late autumn/early spring ❹		Early summer	Aphids
French beans	Spring ❷	After frosts	Summer/autumn	
Runner beans	Spring ❷	After frosts	Summer/autumn	
Beets	Spring ❸		Summer/autumn	
Broccoli	Spring	Spring/early summer	Spring	Cabbageworm
Brussels sprouts	Spring	Summer	Winter	Cabbageworm
Chinese cabbage	After midsummer		Summer/autumn	Fleabeetles/drought
Flowering cabbage	Spring	Summer	Winter	Cabbageworm
Spring cabbage	Summer	Autumn	Spring	Cabbageworm
Carrots	Spring ❸		Summer–winter	Carrot root fly
Cauliflower	Spring ❸	Summer	Autumn–spring	Caterpillars
Celery	Spring	Summer	Summer/autumn	Aphids, cutworms
Swiss chard	Spring	Spring	Summer/autumn	
Chicory	Late spring		Winter	
Corn	Spring ❷	After frosts	Summer	
Cucumber	Spring ❷	After frosts	Summer/autumn	
Endive	Spring/summer		Autumn/winter	
Kale	Spring	Early summer	Winter	Cabbageworm
Leek	Spring	Summer	Autumn/winter	
Lettuce	Spring–autumn ❹	Summer–autumn	Summer–winter	Slugs
Onion	Spring ❺	Spring	Autumn/winter	
Parsnips	Spring		Winter	
Peas	Late autumn/early spring ❹		Early summer	Pigeons
Sweet peppers	Spring ❶	After frosts	Summer/autumn	
Potatoes		Late spring ❻	Autumn	
Radish	Spring–autumn		Summer–winter	Fleabeetles
Spinach	Spring		Summer–winter	
Spring onions	Spring–autumn		Summer–winter	
Tomatoes	Spring ❶	After frosts	Summer/autumn	

❶ In cool temperate climates it is more or less essential that these are started off in a warm light place inside, to be planted out after the risk of frost has passed.

❷ These can be sown outside at the time of the last frosts, but earlier crops may be had if they are started off inside and then planted out later.

❸ Indicates that successional sowing is beneficial because the crop matures rapidly and may then deteriorate. With lettuce and other green leaf salads, it is advisable to make sowings every two to three weeks. With the root vegetables there are usually early- and late-crop varieties, the latter being the ones that can be stored over the winter.

❹ May be sown either just before or just after winter in areas that do not regularly experience hard winters.

❺ Onions are usually grown from small bulbs (sets), but can be grown from seed.

❻ Potatoes are available as tubers (confusingly called "seed potatoes").

the first year

The most difficult part of a garden plant's life is the first year after it is planted. Care at this time will make all the difference. Modern growing methods mean that most plants we put into our gardens have been grown in containers, rather than sold as "bare-rooted stock"; this dramatically reduces the shock of being transplanted. You can plant container-grown plants whenever you like, even in the middle of a heatwave, as long as you keep them watered. Bare-rooted plants are more at risk, as they will have lost a lot of their root system. Perennials establish quickly, within months; woody plants can take much longer.

above **It can take time for a garden to become established, so bare patches of earth may be a feature at first. Careful planning will allow you to fill these spaces the following season.**

watering

The primary need is for water, particularly during hot weather. Water should be directed at the plant's roots, which should be thoroughly soaked. Frequent amounts of a little water, such as is given by a sprinkler, encourage roots to grow near the surface – the opposite of what should happen. Delaying watering until it is actually necessary, and then really soaking the plant, is far more effective, and means that watering need only be done every two weeks in normal summer weather.

controlling weeds

The other main necessity during the first few years is weeding around the young plants. Weeds compete for nutrients and water, and keeping them under control is vital, especially for young trees. Trees and shrubs need the best part of a 3ft-wide clear space around them, free of weeds and perennials.

mulches

A mulch is a surface covering the soil that acts to reduce the spread of weeds and to conserve moisture. Mulches range from plastic sheets to loose materials such as shredded bark. Various brands of plastic sheet mulch can prevent further growth of weed seeds and roots already buried in the soil, but they are not biodegradable. When using sheet materials as a mulch, prepare the soil, lay the mulch and plant through holes cut in the sheet. You can then hide the sheet with a loose covering of bark chips.

Loose mulches, usually of organic origin, will inhibit the growth of weed seed that blows in or is buried in the soil, but will do nothing to stop weed roots from growing and penetrating the mulch. These must be removed before the mulch is applied. Coarse mulches tend to be less attractive, but they offer better protection against weed seed germination and last longer. Loose mulches should be applied after the plants are in place. Planting afterwards inevitably results in soil getting mixed in with the mulch and thus creates an opportunity for weeds to grow.

notebook
planting practicalities

This chapter has explored how to get to grips with the practicalities of planting in your garden. Use the following pages to plan when and how you will get down to work.

choose your edible crops

Use this table to jot down which varieties of fruit, herbs and vegetables you plan to grow. Seed packets and reference books are a valuable source of information when planning your crops to ensure not only that the varieties you grow are most suitable for your purposes, but also that you will have something blooming throughout the year.

fruit/vegetable name	sow	plant	harvest	advantages/ disadvantages

fruit/vegetable name	sow	plant	harvest	advantages/ disadvantages

plan your container planting

Use this space to plan your container planting, following the advice on pages 146–149.

materials required:

plants required:

address book:

your planting diary

Use the planting diary to record what you have done in the garden, and the results that have been achieved. You can use this information the following year to see what changes could be made to the choice of plants, planting times, planting positions, etc.

date	action	progress	comments

date	action	progress	comments

the fact file

If you are bewildered by the range of plants and plant information available, or if there seems to be so much to do in the garden, but you just don't know when to do any of it, this chapter will offer a few pointers to help you on your way.

plant selector

Gardening is most rewarding if you start off with plants that are likely to succeed in your garden. This directory is a list of plants most likely to offer such rewards. It is not a list of the "easiest" plants, which would include many overplanted and dull varieties or the most widely sold, since I have never met anyone who wanted their garden to look like everyone else's.

All the plants described here are long-lived. I have not included annuals or summer bedding plants as there are so many of them and the selection changes radically from year to year. Most of the plants listed here are easily obtainable and are suitable for a wide range of conditions. There is an emphasis on plants for the smaller garden. Inevitably this is a personal list that reflects certain likes and dislikes – but I do have a very wide-ranging taste in plants.

Plants are dealt with here mostly as genera, the first part of the scientific name, with a few suggested individual species or cultivars. Since many genera are very large and varied, the cultivation details tend to be generalizations and are most pertinent to the species discussed. Hardiness in particular varies greatly between species and the indications given apply only to those species mentioned. A good garden plant reference book, such as one of those mentioned in the reading list, is essential.

key to symbols

Size	Hardiness
(as defined at the start of each of the sections)	1 Plants require heated glass.
	2 Plants require unheated glass.
S Small	3 Plants are hardy in warmer
M Medium	regions or situations, or can be
L Large	grown outside in summer but need
	protection from frost in winter.
Aspect	4 Plants are hardy throughout most
☼ Sun	of the United States.
✵ Shade	

trees

Tree planting needs careful thought, with attention given to where a mature tree will cast shade and even where it might fall if blown over.

Large: eventual height above 50ft

Medium: 33–50ft

Small: below 33ft

▸ *Acer palmatum* (Japanese maple)
Slow-growing, deciduous trees and shrubs grown mainly for their red and purple autumn color. Most do well in pots. 'Dissectum Atropurpureum' is a dwarf with dark purple foliage; 'Osakazuki' forms a small tree. *Cultivation:* Well-drained, but moist soil. Shelter from wind and hot sun.
Hardiness: 4   **S** ✵

▸ *Betula* (Birch)
Fast-growing, deciduous trees with distinctive bark. *B. utilis* var. *jacquemontii* has white bark; that of *B. albosinensis* is pinky gray. All cast light shade and have a narrow habit, so are ideal for providing an interesting silhouette in a small garden. *Cultivation:* Any soil, even poor ones. Most tolerate drought and waterlogging.
Hardiness: 4   **S** / **M** ☼

▸ *Chamaecyparis*, x *Cupressocyparis* and *Cupressus* (Cypresses), *Thuja*
Fast-growing, evergreen, coniferous trees. x *Cupressocyparis leylandii* is very fast-

growing and should be used with caution. *Cupressus sempervirens* is the narrow Italian cypress, not hardy in cold areas. Most make good hedges. Dwarf forms are popular in rock gardens. *Cultivation:* Any well-drained soil, even poor ones.
Hardiness: 4

▸ *Ilex* (Holly)
Evergreen shrubs or small trees, slow to medium-growing, with glossy leaves, often with spines; many variegated cultivars are available. Female plants have red berries. *I. x altaclerensis* 'Golden King' is the best yellow-variegated holly. Grown as hedging plants, or clip into standards for formal gardens. *Cultivation:* Any well-drained soil.
Hardiness: 4

▸ *Magnolia*
Fine spring-flowering shrubs and trees. *M. x soulangeana* cultivars have large pink tuliplike flowers. *M. stellata* is shrubby, with white flowers. *M. grandiflora* is a magnificent summer-flowering evergreen. All make good focal points. *Cultivation:* Protect from cold winds and late frosts. Well-drained moist soils are best.
Hardiness: 4

▸ *Prunus* (Cherry, plum, almond, peach, laurel)
Medium-growing deciduous trees and shrubs (see Shrubs) which flower in spring. Check eventual spread when buying for smaller gardens. Pink *P. sargentii* and blush-white *P. x yedoensis* are the perhaps the finest, while *P. subhirtella* 'Autumnalis' flowers in winter. *Cultivation:* Deep fertile soils are best. Many species are disease-prone.
Hardiness: 3/4

▸ *Sorbus* (Rowan, Mountain ash, Whitebeam)
Deciduous, medium-growing trees. All have white flowers in spring, but their main feature is their autumn fruit. *S. aucuparia* has orange-red berries and *S. vilmorinii,* pink. *Cultivation:* Any reasonable soil.
Hardiness: 3/4

shrubs

Shrubs are woody plants with multiple stems and a "bushy" habit of growth, in most cases smaller-growing than trees. Exercise caution when buying, ensuring that you will have room for a mature plant, although they can be kept pruned to a smaller size.
Large: eventual height above 10ft
Medium: 5–10ft
Small: below 5ft

▸ Bamboos
A large group of several genera (including *Bambusa*, *Phyllostachys* and *Pleioblastus*) of evergreen, slow- to fast-growing

shrubby grasses. Their elegant foliage is good for screening purposes, or even for hedging. *Cultivation:* Well-drained but moist soils. Protect from cold and wind.
Hardiness: 4

▸ *Berberis* (Barberry)
Medium- to fast-growing, deciduous or evergreen, spiny shrubs. The sharp spines make them good for hedging, but most are grown in mixed borders for their spring flowers and attractive berries. *B. thunbergii* is popular, many of its forms having purple foliage or a dwarf habit. *B. x lologensis* has orange flowers in spring and blue-black berries in autumn. *Cultivation:* Any reasonable soil that is not drought-prone.
Hardiness: 4

▸ *Buddleia*
Fast-growing deciduous shrubs with masses of small flowers in spikes or globes, much favored by butterflies. *B. davidii* is the most common, with cultivars in purples, pink-mauves and white. *Cultivation:* Any reasonable soil, but are very tolerant of thin, poor ones. Treat as herbaceous in colder climates.
Hardiness: 4

▸ *Camellia*
Evergreen shrubs with glossy foliage that produce flowers in shades of red, pink and white in winter or early spring. They

are good for mixed borders, but can also be used for hedging or grown in pots. *Cultivation:* Well-drained but moist soils. Camellias dislike high alkalinity. Protect from late frosts and wind.

Hardiness: 3

▸ *Ceanothus*

Most of these fast-growing, mostly evergreen shrubs produce blue flowers in early summer, but some, such as C. 'Autumnal Blue', flower later. They are often used as wall shrubs in colder areas. *Cultivation:* Ceanothus tolerate any soil, and are good on poor and thin, dry ones. Protect from cold winds and hard frosts.

Hardiness: 3 🄻 ☀

▸ *Chaenomeles*

Medium-growing, deciduous, often spiny shrubs with early-spring red, pink or white flowers and autumn fruit. Often grown as wall shrubs. C. x *superba* 'Crimson and Gold' has scarlet flowers with yellow anthers. *Cultivation:* Any reasonable soil.

Hardiness: 3 🄼 ☀–❁

▸ *Cistus* (Rock rose)

Evergreen shrubs with a medium to fast growth rate and white or pink flowers, resembling crêpe paper, in early summer. Low-growing ones make good ground cover for dry banks. *Cultivation:* Well-drained soil. Protect from extreme cold.

Hardiness: 3 🅂/🄼 ☀

▸ *Forsythia*

Fast-growing, deciduous shrubs whose brilliant yellow flowers are essential in spring. They are useful for screening. *Cultivation:* Any reasonable soil.

Hardiness: 4

▸ *Fuchsia*

These medium-growing, semievergreen plants make splendid border shrubs, with their pendent red, purple and white flowers. Most flower in mid- to late summer and make effective plants for pots or hanging baskets. *Cultivation:* Any reasonable soil. Hardiness varies greatly.

Hardiness: 2–4 🅂–🄻 ☀–❁

▸ *Hamamelis* (Witch hazel)

Slow-growing, deciduous shrubs that produce scented small yellow or orange flowers in mid- or late winter. *Cultivation:* Well-drained but moist soils; avoid alkaline or thin soils. Protect from wind.

Hardiness: 4 🄼 ❁

▸ Heathers

Medium-growing, mainly dwarf shrubs, including plants in the genera *Calluna* and *Erica*. *E. carnea* flowers in winter; *E. cinerea* and *Calluna vulgaris* in mid- to late summer. Colors range from red and pink to white. All make good ground cover. *Cultivation:* Most need lime-free, well-drained but not drought-prone soil.

Hardiness: 4 🅂 ☀

▸ *Hydrangea*

Slow- to medium-growing, deciduous shrubs with flowers in early to late summer. 'Mophead' or 'Hortensia' hybrids have large, spherical flowers. 'Lacecaps' have more delicate, flattened flowerheads. *Cultivation:* Fertile, well-drained but moist soils. Acid soil is needed for blue-flowers.

Hardiness: 3/4 🄼 ❁

▸ *Lavandula* (Lavender)

Medium- to fast-growing, evergreen shrubs, loved for their scented, usually blue-mauve, flowers and gray foliage. Effective grown as edging plants. *Cultivation:* Full sun and well-drained soil.

Hardiness: 3/4 🅂 ☀

▸ *Lavatera olbia*

Semievergreen shrub with a fast growth rate which bears pink flowers all summer. Useful for quickly filling new gardens. *Cultivation:* Any reasonable soil. Short-lived, but easily propagated from cuttings.

Hardiness: 3/4 🄼 ☀

▸ *Philadelphus* (Mock orange)

Medium-growing, deciduous shrubs with deliciously scented creamy flowers in early summer. *Cultivation:* Any soil.

Hardiness: 4 🄼/🄻 ☀–❁

▸ *Pieris*

Slow-growing, evergreen shrubs with striking, red young growth and white flowers in spring. *Cultivation:* Well-drained but moist acid soils. Protect from cold winds and frost.

Hardiness: 3/4

▸ *Prunus* - evergreen kinds (laurels)

Evergreen laurels (*P. laurocerasus*, *P. lusitanica*) are grown for their foliage, although their beige flowers in early summer are quietly attractive. They make excellent hedging and are tolerant of pollution. *Cultivation:* Any reasonable soil.

Hardiness: 3/4

▸ *Pyracantha* (Firethorn)

Medium-growing, evergreen shrubs with beige flowers in spring and profuse red, orange or yellow berries in autumn. Effective trained as wall shrubs.

Cultivation: Any reasonable soil.

Hardiness: 3/4

▸ *Rhododendron*

Medium-growing, mostly evergreen, small shrubs to medium trees. Evergreen rhododendrons fall roughly into two categories: dwarf forms and larger hybrids with globular flowerheads. Azaleas are generally deciduous, often with scented flowers, such as *R. luteum*. Japanese azaleas are evergreen, low-growing and often colorful. *Cultivation:* Well-drained soil that does not dry out. Most require acid soil and protection from cold winds.

Hardiness: 3/4

▸ *Rosa* (Roses)

Deciduous, usually thorny shrubs with a medium to fast rate of growth. There is a vast number of species, cultivars and hybrids in the genus *Rosa*. "Species" roses have single blooms, flower once a year, and often have a scrambling habit. "Old-fashioned" roses are scented, with heavily double flowers, and many only flower once a year in early summer in colors from red through pink to white. "Hybrid teas" are modern, with flowers in often bright colors and elegant shapes, but they are often scentless. 'Floribundas' tend to be modern, too, but have a more informal habit. "Shrub roses" have an informal habit and are usually scented, but often only flower once a year. (See also Climbers.) *Cultivation:* When grown in situations that do not suit them, roses are even more prone to diseases, such as blackspot, than they are already. A deep soil is essential, and they relish fertile and clay ones. Advice on pruning can be largely ignored; just hack them back when they get too big.

Hardiness: 4

▸ *Syringa* (Lilac)

Deciduous shrubs with a medium growth rate, and large heads of mauve or white, scented flowers.

S. meyeri 'Palibin' is one of the smallest. *Cultivation:* Any reasonable soil.

Hardiness: 3/4

perennials

Perennials are also called "herbaceous" plants, for their habit of dying down in the winter to re-emerge in spring, although a few are effectively evergreen. They reach maturity quickly, and some spread sideways indefinitely, a factor that can be put to good use in ground cover.

Large: growing above 4ft

Medium: 20in–4ft

Small: below 20in

▸ *Achillea* (Yarrow)

These clump-forming perennials with finely divided aromatic foliage produce flat flowerheads in summer in red, pink, white and yellow. *Cultivation:* Any reasonable soil, including dry ones.

Hardiness: 4

▸ *Anemone* (Wildflower)

The spring-flowering *A. blanda* and *A. coronaria* are best treated as bulbs. The latter is short-lived but cultivars of *A. x hybrida* are long-lived with large, white or pink flowers in late summer.

Cultivation: Any reasonable soil.

Hardiness: 3/4

▸ *Aster*

These clump-forming perennials, which come in every color except for the red/yellow spectrum, are invaluable in summer and autumn; Michaelmas daisies

(*A. novi-belgii* cultivars) are colorful but prone to mildew. *Cultivation:* Any reasonable soil, but preferably not dry.
Hardiness: 4

▸ *Astilbe*
Clump-forming perennials with elegant, divided foliage and red, pink and white, plume-like flowers in early summer. Useful for waterside areas. *Cultivation:* Moist, or even wet, soil is essential.
Hardiness: 4

▸ *Campanula* (Bellflower)
A varied group of perennials that nearly all bear blue-mauve, bell-shaped flowers in early summer. *C. cochleariifolia* is a good dwarf rock garden plant; *C. latifolia* is a taller plant for shade. *Cultivation:* Any reasonable, preferably alkaline, soil.
Hardiness: 4

▸ *Carex* (Sedge)
Mostly evergreen, clump-forming, grass-like plants grown for their foliage. Bronze-tinged species, such as *C. buchananii*, are particularly useful for winter color. *Cultivation:* Any soil except very dry ones.
Hardiness: 3/4

▸ *Dianthus* (Carnation, Pink)
The pinks nearly all bear scented flowers in early summer, in shades of deep pink to white. Most are perennial, but a few are biennial. The foliage is often evergreen

and usually gray. *Cultivation:* Any well-drained soils, preferably alkaline, including thin ones. Many are short-lived, but easy to propagate from cuttings.
Hardiness: 4

▸ *Euphorbia* (Milkweed, Spurge)
A varied genus, whose plants range from small perennials to large shrubs, all with yellow-green flowers, usually in spring. *E. characias* is shrubby and useful for early color. *Cultivation:* Any reasonable soil.
Hardiness: 4

▸ Ferns
Dryopteris and *Polystichum* are the most important genera in this group, although *Matteucia* and *Osmunda* provide some wonderful species for moist places. *Polystichum setiferum* is the all-round best, tolerating drier shade. *Cultivation:* Any reasonable soil that does not dry out.
Hardiness: 4

▸ *Geranium* (Hardy geranium, Cranesbill)
These colorful clump-forming perennials flower in early summer. Many are good for ground cover. *Cultivation:* Any reasonable soil that does not dry out.
Hardiness: 4

▸ *Helleborus* (Christmas rose, Lenten rose)
Clump-forming perennials whose winter flowers make them useful border plants. *H. niger* is the white Christmas rose.

Cultivation: Any reasonable soil.
Hardiness: 4

▸ *Hemerocallis* (Daylily)
These clump-forming perennials are midsummer-flowering, with trumpet-shaped flowers in a vast color range: reds, oranges, pinks, yellows and browns. They have broad grassy foliage. *Cultivation:* Any reasonable soil.
Hardiness: 4

▸ *Hosta* (Funkia, Plantain lily)
These clump-forming perennials are grown for their rosettes of broad foliage, often with beige or yellow variegation, or tinged blue-gray. *Cultivation:* Hostas prefer fertile moist soil.
Hardiness: 4

▸ *Iris*
Clump-forming perennials whose distinctive flowers in early summer, and their linear foliage, make them important border plants. The "bearded irises" (*I. germanica*), with evergreen grey foliage, have a wide flower-color range. There are also dwarf spring-flowering species for the rock garden. Some are bog plants, such as the Japanese water iris (*I. ensata*). *Cultivation:* Soil requirements vary: gray-leaved ones like it dry, whereas *I. sibirica*, *I. ensata* and most others prefer moisture.
Hardiness: 4

▸ *Lamium* (Deadnettle)

The silver-splashed foliage of the carpet-forming, semievergreen *L. maculatum* brings winter life to the garden, and in spring they bear pink flowers. They are good for planting under shrubs. *Cultivation:* Any reasonable soil.

Hardiness: 4

▸ *Miscanthus*

Clump-forming perennial grasses which add late autumn and winter interest to gardens. *M. sinensis* has silver or pink plumes on tall stems. *Cultivation:* Any reasonable soil.

Hardiness: 4

▸ *Monarda* (Bergamot)

These slowly spreading perennials bear pink, lilac, scarlet or white flowers in mid- to late summer on upright stems, and look effective when combined with clump-forming perennials. *Cultivation:* Any reasonable soil, but preferably not dry. The spreading habit leaves bare patches in the center, so divide plants in spring.

Hardiness: 4

▸ *Paeonia* (Peony)

The most familiar peonies are those perennials that flower in early summer, with large, sometimes showy, flowers in every shade from crimson to white; but there are also shrubby peonies, such as *P. suffruticosa*, that produce huge flowers in late spring. *Cultivation:* Fertile soil. Slow to establish, and can take several years to flower regularly after planting.

Hardiness: 4

▸ *Papaver* (Poppy)

These perennials or annuals have dramatic but short-lived flowers in the reds, yellows and pinks. Cultivars of the perennial *P. orientale* make good early-summer border plants. The cottage-garden poppy, *P. somniferum* is an annual. *Cultivation:* Any reasonable soil, including poor and seasonally dry ones.

Hardiness: 4

▸ *Sedum* (Stonecrop)

The larger sedums, such as *S. spectabile* and *S. telephium*, are good late-flowering perennials, with their pink-flowered clumps. The smaller ones are succulents for hot, dry rock and roof gardens. *Cultivation:* Border species will grow in any reasonable soil; rock garden ones will grow in anything that offers a foothold.

Hardiness: 4

▸ *Solidago* (Goldenrod)

These clump-forming perennials provide bold splashes of golden yellow in autumn. The smaller species are good for livening up the border, while the larger ones need more space. They are good butterfly plants. *Cultivation:* Any reasonable soil.

Hardiness: 4

▸ *Viola* (Violet, pansy)

Late-winter- and spring-flowering perennials. Plant at the front of the border or in containers alongside bulbs. *Cultivation:* Any reasonable soil, preferably fertile.

Hardiness: 3/4

bulbs

Nearly all bulbs will continue to grow in the garden for many years. Do not remove the foliage after flowering until it has died back; it is busy making food reserves for next year's flowers.

Large: growing above 20in

Medium: 8–20in

Small: below 8in

▸ *Allium* (Ornamental garlic or onion)

This is a large and varied group, varying from low-growing rock garden species, such as the red-purple *A. oreophilum*, to dramatic, tall ones like *A. giganteum*. *Cultivation:* Any reasonable soil.

Hardiness: 3/4

▸ *Crocus*

Most flower in late winter or early spring, in shades of blue/purple, beige and yellow. They can be scattered in the border or grown in grass. *Cultivation:* Any reasonable soil.

Hardiness: 3/4

▶ *Galanthus* (Snowdrop)

Snowdrops establish quickly, forming good-sized clumps. *G. nivalis* is the common one, but there are many others. All have white flowers. Good for planting under deciduous trees. *Cultivation:* Any reasonable soil.

Hardiness: 4

▶ *Lilium* (Lily)

Lilies are summer-flowering, with trumpet- or turban-shaped flowers on tall stems, in a wide color range. The white *L. regale* flowers in summer and has a wonderful scent. Good container plants. *Cultivation:* Fertile, well-drained soil.

Hardiness: 4

▶ *Narcissus* (Daffodil)

Daffodil and narcissus species range from dwarf rock garden plants to the familiar large yellow trumpets. All are white or yellow. Grow in the border or allow to naturalize in grass. *Cultivation:* Any reasonable soil.

Hardiness: 4

▶ *Tulipa* (Tulip)

Tulips come in every shade except blue. There are two categories: large-flowered, upright-growing hybrids, best in borders or pots; and lower-growing species tulips, more suitable for the rock garden. *Cultivation:* Any reasonable soil. Most need hot, dry summers to flower again.

Hardiness: 4

climbers

Climbers can be used to cover any vertical space from walls and fences to archways and obelisks. Some grow rampantly, so check on the eventual size of any climber you decide to plant.

Large: growing above 20ft

Medium: 6–20ft

Small: below 6ft

▶ *Clematis*

The large-flowered hybrids of clematis are popular, but the more elegant smaller-flowered species are becoming more so, such as the spring-flowering *C. alpina* and *C. macropetala* groups and the late-flowering yellow *C. orientalis* and *C. tangutica* types. *Cultivation:* Any reasonable soil, but it is important to provide cool, moist conditions around the roots. Pruning requirements vary.

Hardiness: 4

▶ *Hedera* (Ivy)

Ivies are evergreens that are useful because of their ability to cling to walls, and of their tolerance of shade. *H. helix* cultivars are the hardiest, but *H. canariensis* is one of several species with larger and more exotic-looking leaves. All make good ground cover. *Cultivation:* Any reasonable soil.

Hardiness: 3/4

▶ *Jasminum* (Jasmine)

J. officinale has white flowers in summer; *J. nudiflorum* is yellow and winter-blooming but not scented. *Cultivation:* Any reasonable soil, in a sheltered spot.

Hardiness: 3/4

▶ *Lonicera* (Honeysuckle)

L. periclymenum cultivars come in shades of yellow and pink, and are very fragrant. *L. japonica* is fragrant, semievergreen and very vigorous. Most are good for growing into trees or in "wild" situations. *Cultivation:* Any reasonable soil.

Hardiness: 3/4

▶ *Parthenocissus* (Virginia creeper)

A small group of large-growing climbers that cling to walls and tree trunks. Their attractive foliage turns bright scarlet in autumn. *Cultivation:* Any reasonable soil.

Hardiness: 3/4

▶ *Rosa* (Climbing and rambling roses)

Climbing roses are available in roughly the same range of colors as shrub roses. They vary greatly in height and vigor. "Rambling" roses are large-growing and flower once, in early summer. *Cultivation:* Any reasonable soil is suitable, but deep and heavy ones are best. Prune out old and weak branches during winter. All these roses need support if they are to climb up walls or fences.

Hardiness: 3/4

calendar of maintenance tasks

Many new gardeners are often confused by the plethora of advice about when to carry out certain tasks in the garden. The following chart gives some guidelines about timing, but as in everything in gardening, nothing is set in stone, and if you find you have missed the deadline for planting certain plants or mowing the lawn, try doing it anyway – you will usually get away with it.

season	what plants are doing	tasks	planning ahead
Early spring	▸ First bulbs and flowering shrubs ▸ Beginning of weed growth	▸ Clean up remains of last year's growth of perennials ▸ Remove any weeds	▸ Last chance for seed orders ▸ Buy or order seed potatoes
Mid- to late spring	▸ Wide range of bulbs and shrubs flowering ▸ Perennials making rapid growth ▸ Trees/shrubs forming leaves	▸ Sow vegetables and hardy annuals ▸ Prepare sites for half-hardy annuals ▸ Weed borders, then mulch ▸ Start mowing lawn	▸ Buy half-hardy (bedding and patio plants) from garden center
Early summer	▸ Many shrubs and small perennials flowering ▸ Annuals making rapid growth ▸ First vegetable crops from spring sowings	▸ Plant out half-hardy annuals and vegetables ▸ Hoe weed seedlings ▸ Prune shrubs after flowering if size needs to be restricted	▸ Order fruit trees and bushes from mail-order nurseries ▸ Order strawberries
Midsummer	▸ Wide range of perennials in flower, fewer shrubs ▸ Many weeds setting seed	▸ Deadhead and cut back early perennials ▸ Clear weeds before they seed	▸ Order bulbs and shrubs ▸ Make plans so that land can be be cleared over autumn/winter
Late summer	▸ Wide range of mostly taller perennials flowering ▸ Ornamental grasses, many annuals and half-hardies at best ▸ Cropping of wide range of vegetables and some fruit	▸ Take cuttings of shrubby and half-hardy species ▸ Trim hedges ▸ Treat areas of waste ground with weedkiller before replanting	
Autumn	▸ Final perennial flowers ▸ Berries, autumn leaf color ▸ Autumn bulbs ▸ Many species seeding	▸ Remove dying annuals ▸ Plant spring bulbs ▸ Dig up and protect half-hardy plants you wish to keep ▸ Transplant woody plants ▸ Rake up dead leaves ▸ Bring nonfrostproof containers inside	
Winter	▸ Limited growth of a few winter-flowering species ▸ Dormancy for most of garden	▸ Clear and dig over new areas of garden ▸ Spread compost on borders ▸ Dig over vegetable plots ▸ Transplant woody plants ▸ Reorganize perennial borders	▸ Order seed and summer bulbs (e.g., lilies) and perennials from mail-order companies

plant care troubleshooter

Choosing the right plants for your garden in the first place is crucial to plant health. A healthy plant – one that is growing in a situation that suits it – is less likely to fall victim to any problems. Having said that, garden plants will inevitably suffer from pests, diseases and other problems at some stage. Plant problems constitute a subject of great complexity, and expert advice should be sought on severe or persistent troubles. As with many human ailments, though, time itself is a great healer, and many problems just blow over. It is not worth getting upset about a little black spot here and the odd slug there.

pests

Any animal that eats a plant is referred to as a pest. Many are only a problem at a particular time of year. Some of the most commonly encountered garden pests are slugs, snails, aphids (greenfly, blackfly, etc.), caterpillars and mites.

diseases

This term refers to problems caused by fungi (often microscopic) or bacteria, such as gray mold *(Botrytis)* or black spot. If anything, diseases are even more limited to particular plants at specific times of year than are pests, and are likely to be the result of growing conditions that do not suit the plant. Common disease symptoms are wilting, discoloration and distortion.

physiological problems

Various plant troubles are caused by a deficiency of water or of one of a wide range of minerals. This is a highly complex area, but fortunately most garden plants are very forgiving. Choosing the right plant for the site avoids most such problems.

chemical and biological controls

Many gardeners do not want to resort to toxic chemicals to control pests and diseases unless they absolutely have to. Fortunately, there is now a wide range of relatively safe products on the market, many of natural origin; this means that they will biodegrade safely, but is not a guarantee that they are not short-term poisons, nor that they will not cause allergy problems in a minority of users. Biological controls, which involve the introduction of a pest's natural predator, are also worth a try, especially in the confines of a greenhouse – for example, mealybugs can be controlled by bringing in ladybugs to feed on them.

The following table lists some of the most common plant problems encountered, along with their possible causes and solutions. Bear in mind that no garden could ever be insect- or problem-free – and that only the things that you consider to be problems are in fact problems. What may be an unsightly problem to one gardener can be perfectly acceptable to the next.

symptoms	possible cause	solution
Wilting	**Ⓐ** Drought **Ⓑ** Root damage, often caused by overwatering or rotting in wet winter conditions	**Ⓐ** Water thoroughly. **Ⓑ** Water less frequently or move the plant to a drier position.
Brown edges to leaves	**Ⓐ** Long-term, low-level drought **Ⓑ** Wind scorch	**Ⓐ** Water thoroughly but occasionally. **Ⓑ** Move to a more sheltered location or screen with other plants or fencing.
New leaves turning yellow	Mineral deficiencies, often the result of wrong soil type	Use a fertilizer containing trace elements or sequestered iron.
Small green or black insects clustered around top of shoots	Aphids	Use insecticide spray if problem persists.
Other signs of insect infestation	Can be many and various	Identify insects before treating (or worrying) – they may be harmless. Use insecticide spray if necessary.
Holes bitten in leaves	Usually slugs or snails	Protect young plants with slug pellets or other controls.
White coating on leaves and stems, particularly on roses	Mildew – usually linked with dry weather	Choose mildew-resistant cultivars where possible. Fungicide spraying is possible, but can be ineffective and may be a health risk.
Localized discoloration and spots on leaves	Possibly one of several fungal diseases	Not usually worth worrying about on perennials. Infected twigs on woody plants should be removed and burnt after seeking expert advice.
Sudden death of established woody plant	Possibly one of several fungal diseases that attack roots	Seek expert advice, and replace with a completely unrelated type of plant.

further reading and index

plant reference books

▸ *The Brooklyn Botanic Garden Gardener's Desk Reference* (Henry Holt, 1998) is a comprehensive reference for North American gardeners; however, it includes few illustrations and no photographs.

▸ *The American Horticultural Society A–Z Encyclopedia of Garden Plants* (Dorling Kindersley, 1997) is also very comprehensive, but includes many nonhardy plants.

▸ *The AHS Encyclopedia of Gardening* (Dorling Kindersley, 1993) is very useful for design purposes, but otherwise confusing to use.

▸ *What Plant Where?* by Roy Lancaster (Dorling Kindersley, 1995) is a very useful guide to choosing plants for different situations.

garden and planting design

▸ *The Ultimate Garden Designer* by Tim Newbury (Ward Lock, 1996) and *The Ultimate Planting Guide* by Noël Kingsbury (Ward Lock, 1998) cover the basics of garden and planting design, respectively.

▸ *John Brookes' Garden Design Workbook* (Dorling Kindersley, 1994) is a very useful and systematic approach to garden design by one of its clearest exponents.

▸ *The Gardener's Book of Color* by Andrew Lawson (Readers Digest, 1996) is the best all-round guide to use of color.

gardening on the net

There is an increasing number of websites devoted to gardening, but they tend to offer extensive links to other, mostly commercial, sites, which means that they function primarily as directories. Some have bulletin boards enabling you to converse with other gardeners, and some offer magazine-style articles.

▸ **Gardennet** (www.gardennet.com) offers a directory with links to other sites, but also the premier online garden magazine *Global Gardener*.

▸ **Virtual Gardener** (www.vg.com) offers links to other sites, bulletin boards and some short articles, with links to other online magazines.

▸ **Gardenweb** (www.gardenweb.com) offers a limited bulletin board of garden messages broken down into many categories.

Author acknowledgments:
The author would like to thank Alan and Lesley Rosser for their help with the practical projects.

Text © 1999 Noël Kingsbury
Special photography © 1999 Marianne Majerus
Design and layout © 1999 Conran Octopus
North American text © 1999 Bay Books & Tapes

First published in Great Britain in 1999 by Conran Octopus Limited. North American edition published in 1999 by Soma Books, by arrangement with Conran Octopus.

Soma Books is an imprint of Bay Books & Tapes, Inc. 555 De Haro St., No. 220, San Francisco, CA 94107.

For the Conran Octopus edition:
Commissioning Editor: Stuart Cooper
Editor: Helen Woodhall
Art Editor: Tony Seddon
Special Photography: Marianne Majerus
Picture Research: Rachel Davies

For the Soma edition:
Publisher: James Connolly
Production: Jeff Brandenburg
North American Editor: Ken Della Penta

Library of Congress Cataloging-in-Publication Data on file with publisher.
ISBN 1-57959-042-X

Printed in China
10 9 8 7 6 5 4 3 2 1

Distributed by Publishers Group West

The Publisher would like to thank the following photographers and organizations for their kind permission to reproduce the photographs in this book:
6 Clive Nichols; 7 *left* John Glover (Designer: Susy Smith); 7 *right* Clive Nichols (Gordon White, Austin, Texas); 8 Ron Sutherland/GPL (Designer: Fiona Lawrenson); 9 Ron Sutherland/GPL (Designer: Anthony Paul); 10 *above* Clive Nichols (Designer: Roger Raiche); 10 *below* Clive Nichols (Designer: Sarah Hammond); 11 Marianne Majerus (Designer: George Carter); 14 Anne Hyde; 15 Clive Nichols (Mars Glaisher, Kent); 21 Anne Hyde; 22 Jerry Harpur (Designer: Simon Fraser); 23 Niall McDiarmid/Homes & Gardens/Robert Harding Syndication (Rick Mather); 34 Clive Nichols (Jean Bird); 35 David Askham/GPL; 36 *above* John McCarthy/GPL; 36 *above right* John Glover; 36 *below right* S & O Mathews; 37 *above* Clive Nichols (Christopher Pickard); 37 *below* and 38 *above* Andrew Lawson; 38 *below* Gary Rogers/GPL; 39 *above* and *below* Andrew Lawson; 40 John Neubauer/GPL; 41 *above* Marianne Majerus (Designer: Jon Baillie); 41 *below* Mel Watson/GPL; 46 Jerry Harpur (Annie Wilkes, Sydney); 47 Clive Nichols (Turn end Garden, Bucks); 48 *above* John Glover; 48 *below* Andrew Lawson; 49 *left* Ron Sutherland/GPL (Designer: Anthony Paul); 49 *right* Brigitte Thomas/GPL; 54 *above* and *below* Andrew Lawson; 60 *left* Anne Hyde; 60 *right* S & O Mathews; 61 Sunniva Harte/GPL (Designer G. Pilgrim); 64 Marianne Majerus (Designer: Stephen Woodhams); 74 Andrew Lawson; 75 *above* Clive Nichols (Designer: Roger Platts, Chelsea 96); 75 *below* Jerry Harpur; 78 Marianne Majerus; 79 *above* Andrew Lawson (Designer: David Magson); 79 *below* S & O Mathews (Springlea, Bucks.); 82 *left* Clive Nichols (Daniele Hopkinson, Hampton Court 96); 82 *right* Clive Nichols (Designer: Dan Pearson); 83 Marcus Harpur (Andy Rees, Wingrave, Bucks.); 84 *left* Clive Nichols (Designer: Patrick McCann, Chelsea 96); 84 *right* Clive Nichols (Designer: Elisabeth Woodhouse); 85 *above* Clive Nichols (Designer: Stephen Woodhams); 85 *below left* Clive Nichols (Designer: David Stevens, Hampton Court, 96); 85 *below right* Marianne Majerus (Designer: Neil Collett); 88 Anne Hyde; 89 Jerry Harpur (Designer: Mark Rios, LA, CA); 90 *above* Andrew Lawson; 90 *below* Clive Nichols (Designer: Xa Tollemache); 91 *left* Andrew Lawson (Designer: Anthony Noel); 91 *above right* Harry Smith Horticultural Photographic Collection; 91 *below right* Andrew Lawson; 92 Ron Sutherland/GPL (Designer: Anthony Paul); 93 *above* INSIDE/Met Home; 93 *below* Andrew Lawson (Designer: Mirabel Osler); 96 Marianne Majerus (Designer: Neil Collett); 106 S & O Mathews; 107 *above* Clive Nichols (Barnsley House, Glos.); 107 *below* John Glover; 108 Sunniva Harte; 110 Clive Nichols; 111 Michele Lamontagne/GPL; 112 S & O Mathews (Brookwell, Surrey); 113 Clive Nichols (The Old Vicarage, Norfolk); 114 Steve Wooster/Gardens Illustrated; 115 Clive Nichols (Lakemount, Cork, Eire); 116 Jorgen Schwartzkopf; 117 S & O Mathews (Waldeck, IoW); 118 Marianne Majerus (Designer: Christopher Masson); 119 *above* Clive Nichols (Green Farm Plants/Piet Oudolf); 119 *below* John Glover; 130 S & O Mathews; 131 *above* S & O Mathews (Merrie Cottage, Hants); 131 *below* Marianne Majerus (Clinton Lodge, Sussex); 132 S & O Mathews (Colwell Cottage, IoW) 133 S & O Mathews (Beth Chatto Gardens, Essex); 136 and 137 *above* Andrew Lawson; 137 *below* S & O Mathews; 138 *above* Andrew Lawson; 138 *below* Marianne Majerus; 139 S & O Mathews (12 Rozelle Close, Hants); 142 Andrew Lawson; 143 and 146 *right* Anneke de Leeuw/Taverne Agency; 146 *left* John Glover; 147 Clive Nichols (Designer: Geoff Whitten, Hampton Court 95); 152 Anneke de Leeuw/Taverne Agency
Publisher's acknowledgments: For their help with the projects: **Alan and Lesley Rosser** for the sandpit (owners: **the McGeoch family**) and the gravel garden (owners: **Mr and Mrs Hannick**); **Dennis Fairweather** for the water feature; and **Christopher Winder Joinery** for the decking (garden design by **Fiddeley Landscapes**). Thanks also to **Ali Allen** for modelling and **Keiron Hunter** for building the barbecue.